Food Truck Business: Guide for Beginners

Simple Strategic Plan to Build and Maintain a Successful Mobile Business

Shaun M. Durrant

contained within this document, including, but not limited to, errors, omissions, or inaccuracies.

Table of Contents

Introduction

"I knew that if I failed I wouldn't regret that, but I knew the one thing I might regret is not trying." - Jeff Bezos

Do you stay up at night dreaming of new recipes and owning your own business? You're not alone! There's no dearth of people out there who would dearly love to run their own restaurant, but they just don't have the drive to do so. Notice I said drive, not money or ability or anything else. The will to act is all that matters. The food business is both the best and the worst of businesses to get into.

The positives of opening a food business are many. People always need food and a healthy number of us are foodies. Switch the TV on and you'll see no end to the number of MasterChef type cooking shows.

There's an entire channel, The Food Network, devoted to the topic with cooking shows running all day long. Cooking blogs and cookbooks are some of the most downloaded material on the internet.

Head over to YouTube and there's no end to kinds of recipes and cooking techniques that people demand. Clearly, people love food so it makes sense to give it to them. However, this is also what creates the negatives when it comes to running a food business. High demand isn't a guarantee of success. It's just a start. Just because you cook well, it doesn't mean you're going to be successful. Surveys indicate that the majority of new restaurants close within their first year of operation (*Restaurant Profitability and Failure Rates: What You Need to Know*, 2019).

Why does this happen? Saturation is a major factor. You're not the only one who can see that people are willing to pay lots of money for food and enjoy spending money on it. As a result, restaurants are abundant. Every street corner has a cool looking place that spoils customers for choice. Walk down the average high-end street and you'll find the entire world represented. If your street happens to be in a big city like New York or San Francisco, then this is literally true.

The popular cuisines have sub-cuisines of their own. For example, Indian food isn't just chicken curry anymore. There are many restaurants that serve food from the southern and eastern regions of the country and that food tastes very different from what you might think of as being traditionally Indian. With so many players in the space, it's no wonder that many of them fail. It's survival of the fittest after all.

Running a restaurant is a tough business and your margins are low. Most people who open restaurants are great cooks but it takes a lot more than this to run a business successfully. You need to take costs, margins, and marketing into account. All of this can make your head spin, but it's what the average restaurant owner needs to deal with.

Is your head spinning yet?

Food Trucks

One way of avoiding falling into the restaurant trap is to open a food truck. You've probably seen these everywhere by now. They're takeaway places that operate from the back of a truck, literally. Park them anywhere, serve food, and drive away into the sunset loaded with cash. Reality is a bit different, but the food truck business is booming in America.

People are demanding great food with easy access more than ever. The rise of social media has led to cool food concepts gaining traction really quickly. While some of these influencers take advantage of businesses, food trucks don't have such issues. First off, the concept of a food truck is cool enough to draw passers-by. Second, it's not as if some influencer can simply walk through your food truck and pretend to have eaten there. It's not a restaurant where one can order a glass of water and walk away, after all.

Food trucks offer customers convenience in that they can pick their food up and eat it wherever they want. They don't need to wait for close to an hour at a sit-down restaurant or have to stand in lines to eat greasy food at fast food joints. The quality of a restaurant combined with the convenience of fast food is what makes food trucks such a compelling offer.

Best of all, the economics of a food truck business are a lot simpler to understand for beginners, as I'll be showing you in this book. I'll be taking you from the very first step, why you need a food truck business, to marketing, business plan writing, location scouting, and choosing a good truck.

The most intimidating part of a food truck business is getting approvals. Dealing with the government is always a headache, but in this book, you're going to find that it's a lot simpler than you might think. Besides, there are more important things for you to take care of.

Thinking like a business owner is of paramount importance, but unfortunately most people have no idea what this means. To clarify, it doesn't mean you simply chase money all over the place and cut costs indiscriminately. That's what someone who knows nothing about business thinks it's all about. At its heart, being a business owner is all about taking responsibility and accepting that you being in charge is the best possible thing that could have happened to you.

Why This Book?

What makes me uniquely qualified to advise you about a food truck business? For starters, I've been running a successful food truck for over five years now. Even more importantly, I didn't have anyone teach me through a book like this. I went out there, made a fool of myself, and learned how the business works. There were some tough times but my drive and vision kept me going.

I've always loved food, both cooking it and eating it. Nothing brings more joy to me than to see people enjoy the food I've cooked and then demand more. I found the prospect of running a restaurant daunting. Who wants to be cooped up inside all the time when you could be outside enjoying the sunshine? Besides, I figured that if I opened a restaurant, I'd be married to my location.

I loved the idea that I could always move to another place if one location didn't suit me. I could set up a pop-up restaurant in case there were special events or concerts in the area. This flexibility is what makes food trucks such a wonderful business. In this book, I'm going to show you how it's done.

All I ask of you is a willingness to work hard and believe in yourself. Yes, it's tough running a business but this doesn't mean you cannot do it. You've lived for this long, haven't you? You've dealt with some tough situations by now. What are you afraid of? Get ready to take that plunge and live your dream. You're about to embark on the first steps of a successful food business.

Let's go!

Chapter 1:

The Food Truck Jackpot

Food trucks are potential gold mines if they're run properly. Why is this? I've listed a few of the reasons in the Introduction, but in this chapter you're going to learn more about them. It's not all positives though, there are some negatives you need to be aware of. The success of your food truck business depends on how well you can deal with the negatives.

A truck isn't your only option. There are numerous mobile restaurant ideas you can try if the idea of buying a truck is intimidating you. A food truck owner's daily routine is a busy one, so you've got to love what you do if you want to succeed. The hard work is worth it, and what's more, you don't have to work your truck all the time to make it succeed. These are some of the talking points that this chapter will address.

Why a Food Truck?

There are distinct advantages that food trucks offer when compared to restaurants or traditional food service businesses. The average restaurant manages to load its owners with overhead costs and other expenses before they even begin. Running a restaurant is a serious task, and if you've never run a business before, it's close to impossible to succeed. You need to surround yourself with the right talent before committing to it. The price of failure is high since the costs of setting one up are also high.

Lower Costs

This is not the case with a food truck. Your biggest expense is going to be the truck itself. On average, a food truck's start up costs will run you anywhere from $50,000 to $60,000 (*25 Powerful Food Truck Industry Statistics in 2020*, 2020). This is much lower than what restaurant owners face. With a restaurant, let's look at the number of things you need to purchase before you open your doors.

First, you need tons of kitchen equipment. You'll be serving customers who expect fresh food and you'll presumably be renting a big space. This means you'll need top-notch equipment that can store and cook food. You'll need to hire at least one more cook in the kitchen since you can't do everything by yourself, unless you want to go mad.

Someone will need to constantly wash the dishes and clean the floors. Your restaurant will need to be open for long hours since you'll need to cover more tables in order to make your money back. Look at the life of an up-and-coming chef and you'll see how tough it is. The kitchen is a demanding place and you need to remain in it for long hours to have any chance of success.

Of course, none of this deals with the front-of-house issues. You need an able supervisor who can marshal your waiters and employees to ensure good service. Finding such people is hard. What happens if they quit or do a bad job? You can cook the best possible food but if none of it reaches customers on time, they aren't coming back.

A restaurant's success depends on a lot more than just its food. The added costs increase pressure on owners to focus on many things other than the food. If the restaurant gets its cuisine choice wrong, they'll need to restart all over again, and this means more expenses. With a food truck, you simply change the branding and that's it. You don't need to worry about waiters or cleaning tables.

Thanks to lower costs, your break even points are lower which means lesser hours spent working. You can fix your hours better and keep more of the money you earn. What's not to love?

Brand Recognition

Food trucks also happen to present a great way to opening your restaurant in the future. What's the one thing that all great restaurants have? Brand recognition. If you were to walk along a street filled with a bunch of restaurants, chances are that you'll pick the one that you recognize or feel an affinity for. Choice of cuisine plays into this, of course, but for the most part, people will go with the brands they recognize. It's why Nike shoes sell for five times the price of their cheaper competitors.

In order to build a brand as a restaurant, you need to invest a lot of money in advertising while juggling the other things I highlighted previously. This is a task that's well beyond most restaurant owners. Famous restaurants capitalize on the popularity of their chefs and on the way they cook their food. Some try to make a splash through decor and other innovative concepts. If you're someone who's trying to bootstrap their business, opening a restaurant is not the way to go.

Instead of splashing all that cash on a fixed location, start your business with a food truck instead, and build a reputation in the minds of your customers. The food truck scene is always lively and is well covered by local media since there are so many choices available. A food truck that was serving Greek food last week could be serving Thai street food the next. Consumers are always kept on their toes, and dedicated food truck parks seek to keep the food on offer as varied and exciting as possible.

All of this means you get free publicity without having to do any work. I'm not saying you don't need to publicize your business or invest in advertising. However, you certainly don't need to advertise and invest as much as a restaurant owner would. A roving food truck also generates excitement. Food truck locator apps exist for a reason. Consumers feel as if they're receiving a present of great food when a famous food truck visits their neighborhood.

Call it the ice-cream truck effect or whatever, food trucks generate excitement and buzz when done right. Which means you're building a good customer-base for the future. If you were to open a restaurant down the road, it will likely be packed. What's more, driving your truck to different locations and selling food there is a great way to get to know a location and to test demand in that area. Restaurant owners typically spend time in an area before opening a location. This costs them money since they aren't selling anything.

As a food truck owner, you can park, observe, and earn, all at once. Another advantage is that you'll be running a restaurant without all of the pressure that comes with running one. You cook great food and leave it at that. You don't need to worry about dodgy waiters and other factors that will ruin your customers' experience. You'll get to know how a particular location's legal system operates, and can make a better decision whether you want to open a restaurant there or not.

Passive Income

The restaurant business is a tough one and even successful restaurants require their owners to be present at all times. You cannot outsource the running of a restaurant to a manager without giving up a lot of control and paying them high compensation. Look at the way in which franchise restaurant owners spend their time, and you'll notice that their lives revolve around their businesses, leaving them with very little time to do anything else.

Some people might be happy with this but I'm guessing if you're like most people, this sounds unappealing. A food truck requires work and you'll need to put in the hours. However, these hours are lower, as I mentioned earlier. The other great quality of a food truck is that there isn't much to manage other than a few items. You need to maintain your vehicle, ensure you're abiding by local laws, and serving great food. That's a lot less compared to a restaurant.

This means you can realistically hire a manager and gradually give them more responsibility as you step back from the business. Once you've stepped back enough and have amassed enough capital, you can franchise your business and earn royalties on it. You'll find that doing this is much easier with a food truck than a restaurant.

A restaurant franchise will make you more money, undoubtedly. However, your chances of success are lower with a restaurant. Besides, you'll be faced with the same issues when you open a new location. You'll need far deeper pockets than what you'll need for a food truck. This makes it easier to attract franchisees and earn royalties. Passive income adds up over time, and soon you'll be generating a great income without having to spend time maintaining it.

Pitfalls of Food Truck Ownership

I've listed the advantages but there are some pitfalls you need to be aware of. I don't mean to present food truck ownership as the key to great success. The truth is that it takes a lot of work. You'll need to execute a lot of processes well and constantly evaluate how your business is doing. Many food truck owners get lazy after achieving initial success and this proves to be their downfall. Here are some of the other pitfalls to beware of.

Lack of Planning

There are a few items you'll need to plan before you get your business up and running. Chief among these is your business plan. Your business plan outlines everything that is relevant to your food truck operation. It lists what your locations will look like, what kinds of customers you'll target, and other financial information. Most importantly, it'll also outline when you can expect to make your money back.

This is a crucial point to consider when starting any business. You cannot run a business without capital, and too many business owners fail to consider their true costs. They assume their ventures will be successful from the first day but this is never the case. It takes around six months to a year for your cash flow to stabilize. You need to account for these low sales periods and have enough cash in the bank to pay your bills and maintain your standards.

Without proper planning, you're unlikely to be able to project any of this. Planning is tedious and it isn't exciting. But I'm going to show you how to turn this thought process on its head and make planning something you look forward to. Always remember: If you fail to plan, you plan to fail.

Doing Everything Yourself

Most business owners tend to love having control. However, most business owners also fail. The successful ones learn to let go of their need to control everything and learn to delegate and provide clear instructions to their employees and to the people assisting them in their business. The average person has a warped view of the tasks a business owner carries out.

Common wisdom says that a business owner needs to wear many hats. They need to understand their business, understand operations, understand marketing, figure out taxes and accounting, and also make time to pay themselves. The mistake occurs when the common person thinks that a business owner needs to execute all of these things by themselves. There's a difference between wearing a hat and being a full-blown professional at everything.

As a business owner you need to understand whatever is relevant to your business, in each of those fields. You're not a superhero and aren't perfect, no matter what your dog thinks of you. You cannot hope to become an expert in all of those areas. Instead, you need to focus on what you're good at, and consult with those who know what they're talking about when you need to deal with the other stuff.

For example, if you're seriously considering opening a food truck business (since you're reading this book I'm assuming you are), you're probably well versed in cooking food and understand how to present your cuisine. Let's assume you don't know a thing about marketing, about legalities, about accounting, about setting up a business structure, or even how to run a kitchen. Here's the good news: You don't need to know all of this.

What you need to instead do is learn whatever you can and outsource the tasks that you cannot comprehend. Hire an accountant and use their services to open your business and file your taxes. Hire a junior cook to help you in the kitchen, and talk to or observe other food truck owners to see how they run their operations. If you're deficient in marketing, hire a great graphic designer to create logos and marketing material for you. Have someone create a great website for you, and then also hire a freelancer to incorporate a location tracker.

Whatever you need, there's help for it. The internet has made it so easy for you to find the right people that all you need to do is click a button. So let go of the need to understand everything about everything. Even Michelin starred chefs hire pastry chefs to prepare desserts. Do you think they sit down and prepare their accounts themselves? Do they fix their plumbing issues themselves? They can't even prepare their food by themselves, they need an army of chefs to do so.

So let go of the need to control everything, and instead focus on your strengths. Outsource the rest and success will follow.

Poor Service

You won't have to deal with front-of-house operations when running a food truck, but this doesn't mean you can ignore customer service. To be a successful business, you need to listen to your customers and give them what they want. This is a tough pill to swallow for a lot of restaurant and food service business owners. Why is this? Let's call it the artistic temperament.

Everyone has ideas of what food should taste like and what works best. You might think that salt is overrated and might refuse to add any to your food. However, if the majority of your customers prefer tons of salt in their food, who are you to argue? A famous chef can get away with kicking out customers who want to change the way their food is cooked, but you can't.

This doesn't mean you need to compromise your ideals or serve unhealthy food. However, you need to strike a balance between your artistic side and the health of your business. Compromise is necessary, and you need to remind yourself of why you're running a business. Be passionate about the food you cook and be equally passionate about running a good business. You're probably not the only one who depends on its health.

There are no tables to clean or water to serve so this makes customer service quite simple. The typical food truck customer wants food quickly, and served fresh and tasty. They want their food cooked right and served with a smile. These aren't tough things to do for any business owner. Have fun running your business and your customers will have a great experience as well.

Don't compromise the quality of your food or your cooking to make more money. In the short-term, you will make money, but in the long-term your customers will recognize the drop in quality and will visit some other business. Make sure your food is as fresh and delicious. In the interest of saving time, many food truck owners (and restaurants) cook food beforehand and freeze it. This robs food of its texture and taste. Reheating food in the microwave is no one's idea of cooking.

This is where planning comes in handy. If your menu is elaborate and is full of food that cannot be reasonably prepped beforehand and cooked at short notice, you'll need to change your menu. A food truck customer isn't going to wait for more than five minutes for their food. The idea is to deliver great taste, quickly and conveniently. Tailor your menu to achieve this and your customers will always be happy.

Ignoring Budgeting

This is a mistake you think most business owners would avoid, but it's alarmingly not the case. Many business owners fail to keep track of their receipts and merely guess how much money they're making. It's usually a loss so there's nothing to report there. If you're someone who doesn't keep track of spending and budgeting in your personal life, then forget about opening a business right now. You're not going to magically start budgeting once you open a business.

You'll only replicate what you do in your personal life. If this involves zero tracking, or very loose tracking, you're headed for trouble. A business isn't a game that you should take lightly. You need to be on top of everything. This isn't as hard as it seems, but it requires you to establish processes and consistently practice them.

For example, it should be standard practice for you to deposit the day's take into your business bank account at the end of the day. Much like how kitchens need to be cleaned after the end of the day's service, you need to perform some financial tasks as well. At the end of every month, you need to take stock of how well you did and to plan for the future. You might need to invest more in improvements or on marketing to grow your business.

Cash flow is a challenge for every business owner. You never know when a crisis might occur, either in your own life or with the general economy, and you need to prepare buffers against these. Look at how badly small businesses have been wrecked thanks to the COVID-19 pandemic. It exposed just how unprepared most business owners were. I'm not saying they ought to have predicted how bad the pandemic would get. But, they should have held reserves of cash to prepare for the unexpected.

Just as you save for a rainy day, your business needs emergency cash on hand as well. The rule of thumb in personal finance is to save six months' worth of expenses as cash. Carrying this over to your small business' accounts is an intelligent move and will give you a good margin of safety. Make tracking finances a priority if it isn't already one. Also make sure you incorporate good habits into your personal life.

Carry these over to your business and you'll avoid falling into a debt hole.

Poor Marketing

You cannot rely on the old marketing adage "Build it, and they will come." That's not how marketing works. You need to consciously advertise and target your customers. These days, thanks to advances in digital marketing, it's possible to laser-target your customers. You need to get to know them beforehand (not personally, but their habits), and target them accordingly.

Any business that still relies solely on advertising in print media, and hopes word of mouth spreads is preparing to fail. Your social media strategy needs to be robust. You don't need to keep posting every hour of the day, but you do need to remain active. If social media posting scares you, consider hiring someone to manage your profiles. Many business owners do this and it's an example of how you can outsource the tasks that you don't enjoy.

Marketing is all important these days because many things are competing for your customer's attention. You don't need to scream and shout to be heard, but you do need to invest in marketing and brand creation. A lot of marketing terms will sound like nonsense to you and it's true that marketers can take themselves a little too seriously. This doesn't mean they're wrong, though. Educate yourself on marketing basics and invest in good branding materials. They'll help you stand out more.

If any of this worries you, then just keep reading. You'll gain a good grounding in all of the necessary topics by the end of this book.

Other Options

A food truck isn't the only mobile method of selling food. There are other options available, and it's important for you to review them before you decide to go all-in with the food truck idea. Some of these options might suit you better.

Food Carts

You've definitely seen one of these. In the US, they're mostly associated with hot dog and sandwich vendors. This might lead you to think that's all they're good for, but they can be as versatile as you want them to be. In the developing world, where food trucks aren't as common, food carts are used to sell entire meals.

Some of the examples of meals sold are street snacks that can be quickly cooked in a wok, soup, and ramen bowls. All of these foods are in demand in the US as well, so it isn't as if you can't use one to draw attention. A standard food card is made of aluminum and stainless steel. They're modular and can be used in different ways.

Their portable nature makes it easy to set them up anywhere, and they're a lot easier to obtain permits for. City officials don't have any vehicle related concerns with them, unlike with food trucks, and their portability means even more locations are accessible to them. Instead of parking at a designated spot, you can push your cart right up outside offices and you're guaranteed to attract a steady stream of visitors.

The downside is that you won't do as much business as a food truck will. Carts are smaller and there's only so much food you can handle. However, you can do what many food cart vendors do and recruit someone else to keep bringing you fresh supplies. You can store your supplies either at a designated spot in a vehicle or at your home.

Repurposing a food cart is also very simple. If you try to serve just breakfast food and find that it has no takers, then in the afternoon, all you'll need to do is slide a few panels and you can have a lunch cart. Around 3 PM, you can have a mid-afternoon snack cart serving coffee. This functionality isn't present in a food truck. It's going to look a bit odd if you spot a food truck serving pancakes during the day, Vietnamese cuisine for lunch, and donuts with coffee in the afternoon.

The flip side is that your brand creation opportunities are low, and it's going to be tough to scale directly from a food cart to a bigger business. You can aim to save enough for a truck and build from there.

Concession Stands

These fixed restaurants serve great food and have low overheads. Their locations also ensure that their owners manage to make a good profit. Concession stands are usually associated with movie theaters, but the most profitable ones happen to exist in stadiums. Stadiums these days are fitted out to be used for various purposes. While multiple sports aren't played at the same venue, concerts, and conferences often take place within them.

This makes renting a concession stand during such times a great deal. They're an event-related business, so it's not as if you can rely on them throughout the year. However, if you're looking to earn side-income or test the waters, this is a great way to test your idea. Most concession stands sell junk food, and as people grow more health conscious, there's greater demand for better food.

You can sell healthy versions of local food to draw customers to you. While ethnic food might not be a major draw due to the temporary nature of such stands, it's something to consider.

Kiosks and Booths

These types of food vending locations can be permanent or mobile. Some areas have permanent spaces dedicated to kiosks. Street fairs tend to draw a number of people who frequent food kiosks and booths. You'll find many kiosks popping up near beaches and other leisure areas.

They're not exactly mobile, but at the same time, a food kiosk isn't a permanent structure either. They're usually prefabricated and you can apply your branding to them. Unlike a food cart, you can't switch your branding out. For all intents and purposes, a food kiosk or stand is a food truck without wheels. They have the same appeal but lack the mobility of a truck.

The lack of mobility is replaced by the guarantee of a great location. They're typically leased by the city to operators and the locations always have some festival or occasion taking place that attracts people to them. If driving around or purchasing a vehicle doesn't appeal to you, this is a good option.

Gourmet Trucks

The average food truck is thought to sell cheap and delicious food but there are a growing number of gourmet food trucks. These trucks sell food that is priced even higher than restaurants and attract dedicated fan followings. In many cases, they're used by aspiring chefs to launch their careers.

Food trucks are a cool way to show off on social media, and this helps explain gourmet food truck popularity. Influencers rush to review these trucks, and as a result, if you're an aspiring chef or business owner, you can receive great reviews. There are an increasing number of food truck rallies where different food truck operators gather at a location and people flock to them. The ability to sample food from different trucks is what appeals to them, and this increases the business that the food trucks generate.

Bustaurants

This is a food truck on steroids. Why stick to a food truck when you can buy a bus and seat your customers within it? They're quite popular in Europe where public transport is used more often by people, and they recognize the appeal of converting a bus into a restaurant. In London, old double-decker buses are repurposed as cool restaurants, and they manage to deliver a unique dining experience.

While costs are higher, this is a niche that can be tapped in the US. People will naturally be attracted to a huge red bus that serves food since they've never seen it before. You will have to bear some pioneering pains with regards to permits but it might be worth it. The ability to seat people within your bus, and to operate a takeaway as a food truck usually gives you two ways to appeal to your customers. You'll need wait staff but given the smaller size of the seating area, you won't have to deal with the hassles of a full-blown restaurant.

A Day in the Life

Running a food truck is a full-time job. You can't run it as a side hustle or as a hobby. It's a business and it requires about as much work as a restaurant does. This is especially the case during the early days of running your business. A lot depends on how you structure your menu. If you're going to rely on grilling or baking most of your food, you won't need to devote too much time to cooking your menu beforehand.

Either way, meal prep is involved, and for this reason, you'll need to get started early. If you're opening for lunch, you'll need to start prepping food by 9AM. This means you'll need to wake up at six, meet with your team members and go out and buy food for the day. You'll need to use a commercial kitchen to prep the food and cook it according to your needs.

By 1030 AM, your marketing team must notify your followers of your location, which will have been decided in advance for the week. You'll need to park at your location by 1145 AM and your first customers will start trickling in by midday. The lunch crowd typically lasts till 3 PM after which dinner prep starts. You'll need to clean up and buy food for the night's menu.

Head back to the commercial kitchen and start prepping food by 5 PM. By 7 PM, you'll be back at your location, opening for dinner. This will last until 9 PM at which point you'll probably close. Some owners decide to shift their working hours to serve dinner and after-hour customers. The midnight and after trade is quite lucrative since people are hungry after a night out, and they're willing to pay top dollar for food. Security is an issue and you'll have to be very careful with your cash. However, you'll earn a lot more if you get your location right.

As the weekend approaches, you'll need to start thinking about your location for the next week. There might be events coming up and this is when you'll carry out all of your planning. How much you work on the weekends depends on the kind of trade you're carrying out. If your primary source of income is from the office-going crowd, you're not going to be very busy over the weekend. You can run just one shift at a new location for dinner to try it out. You could also show up at a weekend-only destination, such as a beach or some other event. You'll have to coordinate your social media strategy with your planning and let your followers know where you are.

Treasure the dedicated followers you have since they'll be your biggest champions. Recognize them on social media and give them great offers. This spreads the word and presents your business with a human face. As you can see, there's work to be done. If doing all of this doesn't appeal to you, you're probably better off operating from home and collecting orders online.

Many home-based cooks use this method to bake pies and deliver them to their customers. It's not as if a food truck is the only method of monetizing your cooking skills. You've seen a few of the other options you have. So pursue the ones that appeal to you the most and turn your dream into a reality!

If you're still on board the food truck express, let's move forward and understand how you can create a bulletproof business plan.

Chapter 2:

The Foundation of Your Business -

Why Your Plan Matters

Every business starts with a plan. Unfortunately, most business owners keep this plan in their heads and don't put pen to paper. A business plan is a formal act that conveys you're serious about your endeavor and that you're going to think everything through. Keeping things inside your head or trying to run through mental checklists doesn't work.

You'll be dealing with a lot of issues as you go about implementing your business, and your brain is not going to be able to keep everything in mind. If this is your first business, it's even more important for you to write everything down. A business plan can be intimidating to write, so it's worth taking a look at its various elements and how they help you plan your business' strategy.

Why You Need a Plan

The point of creating a business plan is to force yourself to thoroughly think about everything connected to your business. By writing everything down (or typing it), you'll walk yourself through every aspect of your business in a structured way.

Goals

You cannot figure out if you're doing the right thing unless you have mile-markers that tell you how you're doing. Much like signposts along a road, goals let you know how well you're progressing towards where you want to go. Goals are also a beacon that help you orient yourself once you get knocked about. Make no mistake, you're going to get knocked about as you run your business.

Goals can be long-term or short-term. Ideally, your short-term goals will be derived from your long-term goals. As long as your goals are measurable and time-bound, you're going to progress towards them. A good business plan sets goals that appear unrealistic and that scare you. This is a very important emotion they need to elicit, as odd as it seems.

A goal that is ambitious but doesn't scare you isn't a worthy goal because your mind cannot comprehend it. The sweet spot is when your goal is big enough to energize you but it's also one that you mind comprehends as being outside its current comfort zone. It cannot figure out how to get there and this produces fear. This is how growth happens. Prepare goals that make you uncomfortable. That's what brings progress.

Documentation

A business plan doesn't just help you figure out what your goals are all about, it also helps investors figure it out. You'll need to have a business plan on hand if you want to convince investors to give you money. If you have any plans to franchise your food truck, then you'll need the backing of an investor to expand.

Having a business plan communicates to an investor that you're serious about your business and are committed to it. Think about how it looks to an investor if you show up without a business plan. If you're truly committed to your business, surely you can take the time to write down what it's all about? Your business is a product of your vision so why would you not write it down?

Your business plan also serves as a mission statement to anyone else who works with you. It clarifies how your business operates and why certain processes need to be carried out. If you keep this inside your head at all times, your employees won't know what your vision is. Create a great business plan and share it with those important to the business. It'll help you grow and will motivate everyone.

Strategy

When things get tough, those with a plan get going. I'm taking some liberties with the original quote, I'll admit. However, my point is that a business plan helps you figure out your course of action, in both good and bad times. Anyone can plan for the good times. What are you going to do when customers stop coming to your food truck all of a sudden?

How would you have dealt with the current COVID-19 pandemic? Businesses face risks from unimaginable angles and it's impossible to account for all of them. However, you can always account for the ones that you can clearly identify. This way, you won't be scrambling for cover when the tough times arrive. I can guarantee you that you're going to encounter obstacles you've never imagined existed.

Your business plan will help you ground your response to such situations. Many business owners react in a panic and make things worse. You're smart and will avoid this situation by sticking to your business plan.

Test and Validate

Your business plan is a blueprint for your business. It defines every aspect of it and condenses all relevant information into a single place. Asking for feedback from qualified people is a great way for you to validate your business idea. Validation is a task that most business owners don't undertake. It's tough to put your energy into a creation and then to see it being ripped apart. We don't deal very well with criticism but to improve, you have to seek feedback.

An experienced investor can quickly spot flaws in your business plan and will alert you to them. This is an opportunity for you to fix them and to make your business even stronger. Gathering validation for your idea is essential since business is tough. It's alarming how many prospective business owners underestimate the degree of difficulty they'll face. Your business plan gives you the opportunity to take all factors into account and to face them fearlessly. With the right feedback, you'll easily overcome them.

A Business Plan Template

There are many business plan templates available online. However, a food truck business is a bit different from other businesses. Therefore, your business plan needs to be slightly different. Here are the sections that it needs to contain, at the very least.

Executive Summary

The executive summary is a brief overview of what your business is all about. Brief does not mean a few paragraphs. It needs to extend to at least a page. Most business owners find two pages to be the sweet spot. Your aim with this section is to summarize your business in simple and easy to understand language. It's helpful to complete this section after you've finished the rest of your plan.

That way you can include relevant information (high level) from each section and create a summary. Aim to convey the essence of your business easily. Anyone who reads this section should leave it with an understanding of what's involved. This section also serves as a screen for investors. They'll read it to figure out whether the business makes sense for them to invest in or not. Many investors specialize in certain types of business investments, so the executive summary helps you both avoid wasting one another's time.

Company Description

This section can get a bit boring to read but it's essential information. It deals with the legalities of your company. In here, you'll specify what your company's name is, what the company structure will be, and who the owners and shareholders are. You'll also need to include a brief description (a few lines) of what your business is. If you plan on starting out at a fixed location, you'll need to specify this.

If your locations change, then you should list brief criteria that govern their selection. The style of your food and any relevant information pertaining to that should be included here. You don't need to include menu details. Writing something like "XYZ food truck will serve fresh Vietnamese home-style food" is more than enough.

Market Analysis

This is the first juicy section you're going to deal with. The market analysis section begins with introducing your reader to the size of the market you're targeting. In this case, highlighting relevant statistics about the size of the food truck business, the demand consumers have for them, and trends in the industry is relevant. You could also throw in stats about how restaurants fail, for the most part, and how food trucks are more resilient.

You'll then move on and describe your target consumer. This is also referred to as creating a customer persona. Give your ideal customer a name. Keep in mind you could have more than one ideal customer. Define everything about them as if they were a real person. For example, one of your customers could be Busy Betty who works at a prestigious office downtown and has just half an hour for lunch. She earns over $100,000 per year and has demanding standards.

She frequents expensive restaurants on the weekends and expects high-quality food for lunch, even if it's served to her in a box. She might even send an assistant or an intern to pick her food up. She uses Twitter and LinkedIn a lot, and her friends routinely exchange restaurant recommendations. She loves taking exotic vacations which explain her adventurous taste in cuisine.

Notice that by creating a persona, you're defining methods of targeting your customers. If all of your customers were Busy Bettys would it make sense for you to market on Instagram? Twitter would be a better bet for you. Once personas are done, you'll need to move onto your competitors and describe why you're better than them. Identify potential weaknesses and how you'll fill that gap. Don't make up weaknesses if you can't find any. Highlight your advantages instead.

This is where you'll define your unique selling point or USP. It has to go beyond taste. Anyone can claim on paper that their food is going to taste better. Your food has to taste better, this is a given, so there's no point highlighting it as your primary strength. Your advantage has to come in the form of customer service, ease of access, or through your marketing strategy. You'll tie that last point into a section that will appear further along in your plan, so for now, highlight the key points and direct the reader to the branding, marketing, and PR section later in your plan.

Concept

This is a fun section to write. This is where you'll put your vision down in words. You might have dreamt of what your truck is going to look like and what kind of food you're going to serve. You'll need to highlight key differentiators of your business here. What makes your food special? If you have any experience or pedigree in cooking, highlight them here. "Everyone loves my food" isn't a pedigree. If you've worked in a professional kitchen or have trained under one, mention it here. If you have prior food business experience, highlight it. If you don't have any, focus on consumer demand statistics that show your cuisine is facing high demand.

Explain why it will appeal to your customer personas and which gaps in the market you're targeting. It's also a good idea to explain why a food truck makes more sense than a restaurant. This will help you further describe why your style of food will suit the food truck experience.

Business Operations

If the previous section allowed you to outline the big picture, this one's all about getting into the details. You'll outline how many employees you'll need to hire, what your working hours will be and how you'll get your food out to customers. For example, most food truck owners utilize the services of commercial kitchens to prep and cook food. Some of these kitchens even allow you to store food in them overnight, for a price.

Operations cost you money, and they're essential expenses, so you'll need to account for everything. Even items such as the fuel for your truck and maintenance expenses have to be accounted for. Where will you park your truck? Given that it's your place of business, you'll need to make sure it's securely parked. You can't stick it in your driveway like you would any regular vehicle. Think about all the variables in your business' operations and account for them in this section.

Menu and Costs

This section is self-explanatory. What will your menu look like and how much will it cost you to prepare the items on it? You'll need to account for the time it will take you to prepare each item as well. The time spent cooking isn't a cash cost but it will help you figure out whether your plan to cook your menu is viable or not. Your menu needs to be exciting and written in a way that conveys quality to the customer.

For example, if you were to give guests in Florida a menu that contained food such as Cachorennas, Capirotada, and Chilorio your guests would have no idea what they're about to eat. If you rewrote this menu to read "Traditional fish soup," "Bread pudding," and "Pork seasoned with Chile sauce from Sinaloa," it makes it more likely that they'll order your food. Beginner food truck owners always need help crafting the words on their menu. This is why it's important for you to seek feedback on it from people who have no idea what your cuisine is like. You can literally approach people on the street and ask them if they find your menu appetizing, or you can run polls online.

When it comes to pricing, multiply your food preparation costs by three to arrive at your selling price. This accounts for fixed expenses that can't be broken down unit-wise.

Target Market

This section is usually a subsection within the Market Analysis section. If your target market happens to be a particular neighborhood or cluster of people, listing their relevant statistics as a separate section can be helpful. It depends on how varied your target market is. You don't have to separate this section out, but you need to have this information contained within your business plan.

Location

This is an important section in your business plan. You are a mobile restaurant and have the power to choose your locations. You'll find potentially great spots every day. How will you choose them and filter the best ones for your business? Creating a location scoping plan will help you avoid wasting time searching for spots on the fly. The first step to sourcing great locations is to analyze where your ideal customers hangout and what time of the day they're most likely to frequent food trucks.

There are two approaches to locations. You can go at it alone or you can be a part of a pod. A pod refers to a collection of food trucks that visit certain areas that are planned beforehand. Locations are mutually agreed upon and you'll have to pay a fee to secure a spot in them. You won't have to worry about attracting customers since the presence of a large number of trucks will bring walk-in crowds.

If you do it alone, you can choose your locations as you wish and can capture a greater portion of crowds that frequent a spot. When choosing spots, remember that consistency matters. Customers who like your food will keep returning to you. If you were to change spots every day, this leaves a sour taste that some other truck or restaurant will take advantage of. Some owners plan on serving multiple locations in a single day. This places a huge burden on time management but it's an immensely profitable one if you can pull it off.

For example, you can serve lunch to the office crowd, and then serve late-night food during the later hours between midnight and two in the morning. Remember that permits are a part of your expenses so account for them. In some locations you might have to pay permit and parking costs. For example, downtown Manhattan has huge crowds but you'll also have to pay massive parking and permit costs to operate.

Branding, Marketing, and PR

Let's start with the easy bit. You're driving a mobile billboard so make it stand out. It's worth spending money on a talented graphic designer who can convey excitement and energy to your customers as you drive around. Many food trucks add appendages and other items to give their trucks a unique look.

Next, be active on social media. Instagram is a no-brainer for food trucks so plaster your truck with your handles. Being active on social media is a great way to attract new customers. Don't worry about looking cool. Prompt your customers to tag you in their posts and highlight them in your feed. Create stories regularly so that you stay on top of your followers' feeds. An inactive social media profile can get people to think you're closed, so stay on top of it.

Twitter is a great way to reach local journalists who review restaurants for the weekend arts and culture pages. You can also reach out to freelance writers in your area via LinkedIn or Twitter and ask whether they'd be interested in writing a story about you. Websites such as Yelp and food truck directories also help spread the word about you, so make sure you're listed on them. Prompt your customers to leave reviews since they'll drive more people to check you out.

Company and Management

This section is for you as much as it is for any investor. Running a business is stressful and you need to think about how you're going to structure your company. Many first-time entrepreneurs go into business with a partner. This person is usually a friend or a spouse. Think about how running a business will affect your relationship and whether it's worth risking it. You're going to face a lot of stress and if you feel that your partner isn't pulling their weight, you're going to have to deal with even more stress.

Investors prefer to put money into ventures that have more than one founder. This helps them manage the risk of having one founder fall ill or give up on the business. If you're looking to source investment, it's best to work with a partner. A co-founder can also help you handle the areas of your business you're not comfortable with or lack expertise in. For example, if you're great at cooking food but can't make head nor tail of marketing, having your co-founder take care of that part of the business makes sense.

The key is to choose wisely. Don't let emotions override logic. Your co-founder needs to bring value to the table and needs to have proven skills in the areas they'll be handling. The two of you need to be able to work together and support each other. If you're working with a partner, your business' structure will need to protect both of your rights.

You can fold this section into the "Company Description" section or break it out separately.

Financial Plan

This is the meat of your business plan, along with your marketing strategy. The first item to address is your sales forecasts. How many meals will you sell every day and what will be your customers' average spend? Account for seasonality as well. People will spend on different items depending on the weather. Coffee will sell better than ice cream in winter, for example.

Next, what are your gross margins? You can calculate gross margins by subtracting your cost of purchasing materials (COGS) from your average sales and dividing this number by your sales. For example, let's say you have five menu items and it costs you $300 to purchase raw materials for them every month. If you plan on selling those items for $900, your gross margin is (600/900) 66%. A gross margin of 50% or more is considered great.

You'll now need to figure out your net margins, to do this you'll have to include operating costs and other expenses to your COGS. Your expenses include salaries, insurance, fuel costs, permits, vehicle loan-payments, commercial kitchen costs, packaging, vehicle maintenance costs, and so on. Obviously, specific costs depend on how you'll run your business, but make sure you account for all of them.

Subtract your total costs from projected sales and divide this number by your sales to arrive at your net margin. For example, if your monthly costs add up to $1,000 and your COGS is $1,000, your total expenses are $2,000. Let's say your sales are $3,000 per month. This means your net margin is (1000/3000) 33%. Truth be told, this is a pretty high net margin, and it's unlikely you'll hit this number in the real world. A food truck business typically has margins around 10%. This means if you sell $10,000 per month worth of food, you can expect to earn $1,000 in profits.

Let's break this down a bit to see how realistic this is. $10,000 per month in revenues equates to (10000/30) $333 of sales per day. Let's say you operate only during lunch hours between 12 PM to 3 PM. If your location draws enough people in so that you can serve 12 people per hour, you'll serve (12x3 hours) 36 people per day. The average purchase price for a food truck is usually $10. This is the cost of a drink and a food item.

This means your sales-per-day will be $360 which is above the $333 you need to hit to achieve $10,000 per month. There's also the fact that these are extremely conservative estimates. 12 people per hour is one person served every five minutes. During lunch hours at a good location, you'll be serving close to one person every minute. You can't expect huge volumes every day of the year, but 12 people per hour is an extremely conservative estimate. If you can make your business work by serving such a small number of people, it's going to be hard to fail.

$1,000 per month might not sound like a lot but remember this is over and above the salary you pay yourself. So it's not as if you're going to live in a cardboard box to run this business. Run this simple analysis for all of your proposed locations and break them out like this. Your investors will see you're serious about your business.

Once your gross and net margins have been calculated, you'll need to list startup costs. These are one-time costs you'll need to begin doing business. There's the cost of your truck, the fit-out costs, and other permits you'll need. It's safe to assume that you'll need $100,000 to begin doing business. This sounds like a lot, but you can always apply for a business loan. Your loan will call for you to make monthly payments and this will be deducted from your net margin.

Drawing a loan of this size will help you buy your truck for cash and avoid having to make expensive monthly vehicle payments. Those loans carry higher interest rates than bank loans, so your monthly payments will be less. If you want to avoid drawing a loan, you can choose to finance your vehicle purchase, which will greatly reduce your upfront costs. Check out used food trucks to get even better deals.

At this point, you have three important items:

- Startup costs
- Monthly revenues
- Net margin (profit per month)

Using these three numbers you can create two forecasts. The first is the profit/loss forecast. List your costs in a column per month. For example, the first month will incur startup plus COGS and operating expenses. The second month will have just COGS and operating expenses. In a column next to it, list your monthly revenues. The third column will list the difference between your revenues and costs (revenues minus costs) to give a monthly figure.

Your first month will list a negative profit (a loss) while the remaining months will list a profit. Add these profit numbers together to determine how long it will take you to break-even. For example, let's say the first month's loss is $5,000 and subsequent months profits are $1,000 each. This means it'll take you five months to break-even.

Something to keep in mind is that your vehicle purchase costs will not be included in this calculation. This is because it's a capital expense (expenses made to purchase assets), and these don't figure in profit and loss statements. The place they go into are cash flow statements. These are exactly the same as profit and loss but the objective is to project cash flows every month. You won't have to calculate break-even expenses here.

If this is leaving you dizzy, I recommend purchasing a business planning tool such as Liveplan that will help you input numbers and will do the heavy lifting for you. Do not neglect this portion of your plan since it's the most important one.

As you can see, all of these sections require you to prepare beforehand and think about your business from different angles. The result is you'll learn your business better and will have a ready made document that outlines the key points of your business. As your business grows, some of your estimates will change. In fact, when you're starting out estimated regarding revenue and cash flow will be off. It's better to underestimate these numbers rather than overestimate them. This way, you'll receive a nice boost when the real numbers come in.

Niche Research

The biggest task ahead of you is to research your niche. This will clarify your marketing plans, your customer personas, everything else related to your menu, and how you'll present yourself. Niche research combines many different points of research into it. For starters, let's define what a niche is. A niche is an interest or a commonality that many people share.

The key word to focus on is "many." If there aren't enough people interested in something, there's no way to monetize that interest. The cuisine of New Caledonia might be mouth wateringly good, but if no one's interested in it, or has even heard of it before, you're not going to earn a profit. You might think that introducing this cuisine will help you gain the first move advantage. However, pioneers rarely make money. Look at the successful businesses out there and you'll see that none of them were the first. They've grown so big that we've simply forgotten everyone else that came before them.

In order to select a good niche, you need to find a sweet spot. This spot is where you'll have enough people interested in your food to visit you, but you'll be narrow enough to differentiate yourself from the competition. For example, you could open a burger van but this is not a niche you can easily differentiate yourself in. Why are your burgers better or how are they different from the others? Why should a customer buy your burgers and not head over to Five Guys or McDonald's?

Your choice of niche ties back to your USP. It's tough to nail this down at first but it's essential you keep working at it. Examine other food truck businesses to figure out what their USPs are. This will give you a good idea of your own proposition. A USP can come from a thorough examination of the market.

Questions to Ask

Market analysis is important if you wish to make a success of your business. Here are some relevant questions you can ask yourself.

- What are the existing options available in the market? Research options at your locations.
- Are there any gaps? Is every place offering burgers but is anyone selling burritos? Alternatively, is every place a sit-down restaurant and people want quick takeaways?
- What is the competition like? How many food trucks, vendors, and restaurants are there? Which restaurant witnesses the highest traffic?
- How are customers currently handling food from mobile vendors? Do they eat them in the street or do they head back to their homes/offices? What is their behavior like? This can give you packaging ideas.
- Which times of the day have the highest demand? Which days of the week are the best for local establishments?

Make it a point to sample all of the food available at your location. You don't have to eat at the fancier places since they're not your competitors. Instead, sample food from everyone who is likely going to become a competitor. Notice how long their lines are and whether people are willing to spend time standing around for their food. Every market has gaps that are invisible to current operators. You have an outsider's advantage so make use of it.

You could ask some of the vendors these questions but be prepared to get stiff-armed. Some establishments will let you know relevant points, but don't expect them to open their books up to you. If you're great at building relationships with people, then you can expect this approach to pay dividends. Once your research is completed, sit down and compile lists of everything you saw.

Now connect the dots. A gap in the market might be readily visible or it might take some digging to get to. Match this to your own skill set and see if you can plug the gap. For example, there might be a ton of Mexican food vendors in your area, but are there any vegan options? What is the demand for vegan food like at your location? These are just a few questions for you to consider.

You could even switch up the type of food you serve while remaining within the cuisine. You could serve only Mexican desserts or Mexican breakfast food. Smoothies and juices are a great option and people will buy them to complement their meals. Think outside the box and don't get stuck on a single idea. You might envision making burritos, but if the market doesn't want them, consider making smoothies or desserts. It's not as if your cooking skills center around just one type of food.

Your Name

Naming your business is crucial, so spend time choosing a catchy and memorable name. Your name should convey what food you're serving and should ring a bell in people's minds. It should also be easy to pronounce. Many restaurants make this mistake. How many times have wandered around the fancier parts of town and have run into a restaurant named "Au Relais de l'Entrecôte?" That's a real restaurant by the way.

It's famous in Paris, but retaining this name in the English-speaking world poses challenges. No one can pronounce it for starters, and fewer can understand what kind of food they can expect from such an establishment after reading the name. It does very well in big cities like London and New York, but it does so despite its name. But, it is a famous Parisian bistro. Expecting your fledgling business to overcome an incomprehensible name is a stretch.

Your name should be non-controversial. No matter what your political or religious opinions are, don't incorporate them into the name. Also, avoid using geographical references that might tie you to one place, although you can sometimes break this rule. For example, Kentucky Fried Chicken managed to expand despite mentioning a location's name. Don't zero in too much on a certain style of food since this might pigeonhole you into a niche that you cannot expand out of.

Make sure your name isn't trademarked or you'll attract biblical penalties. Brainstorm different names and run them past your friends and family. Choose the one that feels right. There's no clear method to picking the best name all the time. You need to trust your intuition and rely on logic as well. Avoid getting too creative with your name.

For example, Mercedes-Benz is a person's name and has nothing to do with cars. It's a bit like a company named John Smith becoming popular for its cars. Apple doesn't sell apples and Facebook does a lot more than just capture pictures of your face. Good examples to emulate are Twitter and Reddit. On Twitter, users tweet their thoughts in sharp bursts and just like the bird's output, most of the content is nonsensical. Reddit is a take on "read it" and it clearly describes what that social media site is about. It's text-based and allows users to choose which subjects they want to read about.

Emulate these names. They describe what the service is about and add a creative spin to it. For example, our Mexican food truck serves burritos, tacos, enchiladas, and the other usual suspects. You could pick a name like "Pablo's Burritos" but this is quite plain. A name like

"Hot Tamale" could refer to almost anything, including adult entertainment venues. How about "Holy Guacamole!" or "Chicky Chimichanga?" Brainstorm ideas and run surveys. Stick with the one that feels best.

Chapter 3:

Getting Your Ducks in a Row -

Finance Essentials

When you're starting your business, your first priority will be to arrange money to get started and pay those startup costs. Many business owners fail to look past those initial costs and set themselves up for failure down the road. They borrow too much money upfront and create unsustainable cash-flow burdens for themselves. Once the business goes under, they think there was something wrong with their food or with their branding. In reality, it was their capital structure that was all wrong.

It's a lot like borrowing money to buy a house. You can put down just 3% and move in but your monthly mortgage payments are going to be high. This makes it critical for your income to remain steady. If you'd instead taken some additional time and saved 30% to put down, your monthly payments will be much lower and you'd have greater peace of mind.

Debt is a great tool, but like every tool it can be used incorrectly. What's correct for one person might be incorrect for another. Unfortunately, there's no clear-cut path, and you'll need to run the numbers on paper and determine what you're most comfortable with. Don't borrow money and think you'll somehow manage to make payments in the future. This is what failing business owners do. Kicking the repayment can down the road is never a good idea.

Startup Costs

A food truck costs less to get up and ready compared to a restaurant. However, this doesn't mean you can get started without any money in the bank. That's just being unrealistic. To run a successful business, you have to have capital. Much like how you need air to survive, your business needs capital and cash in the bank to allow it to prosper. If you're short of capital, you can structure your business in such a way so as to make it a success. However, don't create a capital structure that makes it tough for yourself.

Here are some of the costs you'll encounter when starting up.

Vehicle Cost

This is your biggest expense. Food trucks don't come cheap and you might have to borrow money to purchase even a used one. A food truck isn't a van that has some microwaves bolted into it. They're purpose-built commercial kitchens on wheels and require serious investment. A new food truck can cost you anywhere from $75,000 to $150,000. A used food truck's price starts from $50,000 (*How To Start A Food Truck Business: A Cost Breakdown - Innovative Ideas & Solutions*, 2018).

A method of saving money is to buy a food trailer instead of a truck. These can be hitched to the back of a truck and you'll be able to tow them into your preferred spot. Trailers cost between $15,000 to $50,000. While they're cheaper, you'll be cramped within them. Also, you'll need to figure vehicle parking costs and towing costs. However, the upfront cost savings can turn an unprofitable idea into a profitable one.

On average, it's recommended that you set aside $75,000 to $80,000 for truck purchase. This will land you a good truck that will be reliable over the course of two years, assuming regular wear and tear. If this is exorbitant for you, consider renting a food truck. Commercial (or commissary) kitchens offer food truck packages and you can rent space in the kitchen along with a truck for a monthly price. Packages typically cost $2,000 to $3,000 per month. You can negotiate kitchen use as a part of the contract.

You'll earn a dollar amount as credit every month in standard packages and can purchase more hours as your business grows.

Kitchen and Serving Equipment

Not all food trucks come with built-in appliances. Depending on your needs, you can specify that your truck has a grill or an oven, but most trucks require you to install appliances within them beyond these. Appliances cost money and you can expect to spend an additional $2,000 upfront purchasing and installing them.

To save upfront expenses you can lease appliances. Commissary kitchens will put you in touch with companies that can provide these services. It's best to buy appliances and other serving ware upfront. They're not huge expenses when compared to the truck and borrowing money to pay for them doesn't make sense. By opting for monthly payment plans, you're paying interest on those appliances and this isn't an optimal use of your money.

Licenses and Permits

According to the U.S. Chamber of Commerce, food truck operators need to spend $28,276, on average, every year on permits, licenses, and other legal requirements (*Here Are Need-To-Know Food Truck Costs (and How to Save Money)*, 2020). There are different types of permits you'll need. The first is a business operation's permit that you can apply for with your municipality. Other permits fall under the following category:

- Safety and hazards
- Food safety
- Vehicle
- Zoning
- Employment

Aside from these permits you'll also need to pay for parking permits and insurance. Some cities are friendlier to food trucks than others. Boston is the most expensive when it comes to food truck licensing while Philadelphia is much friendlier. Here are the rough costs you can expect to pay (*Here Are Need-To-Know Food Truck Costs (and How to Save Money)*, 2020):

- Business Registration: $75 to $150
- Vehicle Registration: $75 to $100
- Health Permit: $250 to $1,000
- Fire Permit: $100 to $150
- Food Truck Application and License: $100 to $500

Business insurance will cost you around $2,000 to $4,000 per year and will cover all forms of liability, from customers getting food poisoning to employee injury liabilities. There are also parking fees to contend with. You can expect to pay between $250 to $1,000 every month. Your commissary kitchen will charge you around $500 to $1,200 every month.

Popular events and festivals invite food truck applications and these opportunities are usually extremely lucrative. Event managers collect fees from service providers. A food truck can expect to pay between $500 to $1,000 per event. Some events take a slice of the revenues you earn. This is usually the case with bigger festivals or events, such as New Year's festivals where crowds will be huge.

Startup Inventory

You need food to get started and this is going to cost you money. Estimating food inventory costs can be tough at first. The method is quite simple in reality. Look at all of the raw food material you'll need to cook your menu, and estimate their per serving cost. For example, if one burrito contains one serving of meat, one of rice, half a serving of beans, a quarter serving of cheese, sour cream, and guacamole, you can arrive at the cost price of one burrito easily. Look at the price of a larger quantity of your ingredients and divide costs accordingly.

How many servings of guacamole are in a container? Divide the cost of the avocados and other ingredients by the number of servings, and then divide that number by four to arrive at your unit (per burrito) cost. How many people do you expect will buy food from you? Multiply your unit costs by this number to arrive at your monthly inventory costs. To start, it's best to have four to five days' worth of inventory on hand.

You'll also need cookware such as pots, pans, and spatulas. These will cost you around $500-$1,000, upfront. You'll need to decide how your food is going to be served. If you'll be providing boxes, you'll need to buy these beforehand. Your costs depend on the quality purchased. Like with food, it's best to have four to five days' worth of inventory on hand, at the very least.

It's tempting to buy the freshest ingredients but these cost a lot of money. You don't need to forage for food from the dumpster but you need to balance quality with costs. Many restaurant owners fall into this trap and buy the most expensive ingredients instead of focusing on creating quality from cheaper ingredients.

Operational Costs

Operational costs include gas, permits, maintenance, and salary costs. You won't pay all of these upfront, but it's better to set aside at least two months' running costs in your bank account. If you're borrowing money, interest payments are also a part of operating costs. The biggest upfront operational cost will be installing a point-of-sale (POS) system. These days, POS systems come in many varieties. The older systems come with hardware and can provide you with all kinds of reports. As contactless and digital payments rise, mobile POS systems, such as Square, are increasing in popularity. All you need is an app to accept payments.

Your customer will scan a QR code from their phone, and use an eWallet to transfer money to you. In reality, you'll need a solution that is somewhere in between these extremes. You will need to rent card payment machines from your bank, and will need to keep a track of all of your receipts for tax purposes. You will pay an upfront cost for the hardware and a monthly cost for software maintenance. This will cost you around $75 per month.

Labor Costs

Labor costs are usually included under operating costs, but it's worthwhile to highlight them separately. The wages you pay your employees will vary depending on your location, but you can expect to pay between 30-35% of your operating costs as salaries and labor expenses. This is just an average figure so you'll need to conduct research into your local market to figure out exact costs.

Marketing

You'll need money to spread the word about your business. A website is the minimum requirement and, fortunately, these are inexpensive. But, you might need help with social media management. Remember that you need to be active in your outreach, as opposed to hoping people find you. Expect to spend at least $1,000 in marketing and promotional activity during the first month.

Consider implementing a loyalty program. This usually gets customers to keep coming back to you. Offering a free drink after five orders or a free meal after 10 purchases are common ways of promoting loyalty. Allowing your customers to order online and having them pickup your food is a great way to expand your customer base. Customers use online food delivery services such as Uber Eats to pick up food, so consider signing up with them.

All of these costs add up, and it can be intimidating to try to figure out where you're going to raise all the money you need. You have a few options when it comes to this.

Raising Capital

All businesses have two choices when it comes to raising capital. They can raise money through debt, or by selling equity. Debt is the financial term for borrowing money through loans. You can approach a person or a bank for a loan. Given that your business is new and starting up, a bank is your best bet. There are pros and cons of using debt to fuel capital growth.

The advantage of using debt is that you can cover interest payments monthly from your revenues. This helps you get started quickly without having to pay a large sum of money upfront. More importantly, you don't give up any control of your business. You get to own your business in its entirety, and don't have to split the profits with anyone else. As your business and its profits grow, this point will be extremely relevant for you. You'll be adequately compensated for all of your efforts.

There are disadvantages to account for. For one thing, the loan that the bank provides you needs collateral. Collateral is usually a home or some asset that you own. If your business doesn't work out, you'll end up losing the asset. Are you willing to put your home on the line to fund your business? Many business owners make this choice and have sleepless nights when their business begins to perform badly. You also need to be able to qualify for a business loan.

Since the 2008 crisis, banks have tightened their purses considerably, thanks to government regulation limiting how much risk they can absorb on their books. As a result, first-time business owners that need capital will find themselves being shut out, which is exactly the opposite intention of the laws that governments passed. Banks as a result, end up lending money to the people who need it the least. Consider the following questions before opting for debt financing:

- Will I qualify?
- Am I willing to lose my home or asset?
- Are the monthly payments affordable?
- Can I borrow more money if I need it?

If debt financing doesn't suit you, equity financing is your second option. Equity financing doesn't place a strain on your cash flow every month. However, it involves you carving out a portion of your company and selling it to someone else. Therefore, you're not paying a fixed amount of cash every month, but are paying someone a cut of your profits.

Equity investors assume more risk and want some degree of control in return. This means you need to choose your partners carefully. Experienced equity investors know enough to give you the money, ask for minimum cash flow every month, and let you run your business. Many investors happen to be inexperienced, however. It's unfortunate, but many people with money don't know what to do with it and end up investing in businesses they don't understand.

They don't understand that businesses fluctuate, and they may start interfering in your daily tasks. Such investors aren't worth the time, no matter how much money they bring to the table. Here are some pertinent questions to ask yourself before opting for equity investment:

- Is my concept appealing to private investors?
- Am I willing to give up a portion of my company and allow someone else to control it?
- Am I willing to give someone else access to the company's financial information?
- Am I willing to share the profits of my hard work?

Think about that last point deeply. You might be focusing on just the mountain of cash you need to raise right now. What if your food truck begins to earn you $10,000 in profits per month through franchising and other monetization methods? Would you be willing to give up 50% of those profits to an outside investor? Especially when this investor gave you money just once and hasn't done anything else since then?

Structuring equity agreements is crucial, and you need to use the services of a lawyer to help you navigate shareholder agreements. There are many clauses that can derail you so take our time with it. You don't want to lose control of your company because you neglected to read a few clauses.

Sources of Debt Capital

The preferred source of debt capital are banks, but as I mentioned previously, they're less than willing to fund you if you don't have experience. If you have prior experience in the food industry, then you stand a good chance of getting approved. Given that banks have tightened their purse strings, online lenders have become a great alternative. The number of loans provided by FinTech firms is constantly increasing, and this is especially true for small businesses.

The average size of a bank loan to a business is around $1 million, whereas FinTech firms come in at $100,000. Clearly, the latter is better suited for your needs. Firms such as Funding Circle, BlueVine, and OnDeck provide small businesses with quick approvals. You can expect to get funded within three days after submitting your documents. These firms don't have to adhere to strict government regulations since they don't accept deposits. As a result, they can be more liberal with their loans.

The collateral requirements vary depending on the lender. Usually, a business lien is required. This means if you default on payments, the lender can seize your business assets and auction them. For instance, your truck can be seized and sold to recover money by the lender.

If you don't wish to borrow from a private lender, you can opt for a Small Business Administration or SBA loan. These are government loans that are issued through approved lenders. SBA loans usually require borrowers to pay 30% upfront, so you'll need to have some cash on hand. However, their interest rates are lower than private small business loans and the collateral requirements aren't as onerous. After all, the government can take a hit or two and doesn't need as many guarantees as a private lender does. There are different SBA programs, so make sure you check with an approved lender before applying for a product.

The final source of debt financing is your friends and family. A debt agreement might work better with them than an equity agreement, since the last thing you might want is Uncle Jim questioning the quality of your sauces. You will need to structure a note that specifies repayment terms. You'll need the services of a lawyer to do this. You can implement the same approach with a private investor, but you'll need to know them well to pull this off.

Merchant cash advances and credit cards are other options you have. Both of these are impractical. First, merchant cash advances lend you money at exorbitant rates. The interest rates on those loans typically work out to more than 100%. If you borrow enough money, you'll never recover from the debt hole you'll create. Never utilize this option. Credit cards don't charge such ridiculous interest rates, but their rates are still high.

The interest rate of an average credit card is 17% and you can never make money borrowing cash at these rates. Use them for small purchases but never borrow large sums from them.

Sources of Equity Capital

The most obvious source of capital is your personal savings. Everybody's personal financial situation is different. However, don't make the mistake of sinking everything you have into your business. You should always have enough to cover emergency expenses and living expenses for at least six months. If you happen to have wealthy relatives or know a wealthy individual, you could offer them an equity stake in your business.

Another approach to consider is to partner up with someone who can handle the tasks you're not proficient at. I previously cited the example of someone else handling marketing while you handle the food. Your co-founder can contribute cash to your business account and you can divide your equity stakes on the basis of your cash contributions. Obviously, you'll want it to be 50/50 for it to be equitable. However, you can negotiate equity stakes depending on how much work either of you does.

Do not give an outside investor a majority stake in your business. For example, someone might offer you all the cash and agree to give you sweat equity in your business. Sweat equity rarely exceeds 20% so this deal is simply not worth it for you. Even if you agree to such a deal, make sure you negotiate decreases in equity down the road. After your business reaches certain profit thresholds, the investor decreases their stake gradually and you increase yours. This way, the relationship has the potential of becoming equitable over time.

A method that is becoming more popular as time goes on is crowdfunding. Crowdfunding is technically neither equity nor debt, but it's a great way for you to test your business idea with potential audience members. The way it works is you put together marketing material and launch a campaign on a crowdfunding platform such as Kickstarter or Indiegogo. You will set a campaign target and if it's hit, you'll receive the money. If the target isn't hit, you won't receive anything, and you'll know that your idea doesn't have traction.

Typically, crowdfunding contributors are compensated with rewards. For a food truck, sample rewards might be a special delivery of food for different contribution levels. A $5 contribution would result in their names being printed on your truck, a $10 contribution could result in a menu item being named after them, a $20 contribution would lead to a t-shirt, and a $100 contribution would lead to a menu item plus a special gift from you. You can't ship fresh food to them but you can send them a variation of your recipes. For example, if you're serving Mexican food, you could ship them a batch of your very own guacamole in a bottle.

Crowdfunding success isn't easy. You will need the assistance of a marketing firm that specializes in such campaigns. Typically, they'll charge you a flat fee or take a cut of the money you raise. The latter option can be especially lucrative since there is no ceiling to the amount of money you can be given. If your goal is $100,000 but you raise $500,000, you get to keep the cash. Choose to work with such result oriented firms.

However, your concept and food needs to be exciting enough for these firms to sign up. So spend some time refining your concept and creating your business plan. It will help you land both debt and equity financing.

Managing Costs

The best way to attract financing offers is to keep your costs and startup capital low. You can do this by tailoring your menu and operations to ensure low costs. Here are some of the methods you can employ:

- Use seasonal ingredients - Why seasonal? Because they're cheaper and are most likely produced locally. Positioning yourself as a sustainable restaurant will score you points with customers.
- Go easy on inventory - You might be tempted to rush out and buy all the ingredients you need and stock up. However, remember that at first it's better to take it slow. It's better to sell out than to have leftovers.

- Ask friends and family for help. They're your biggest supporters and will be willing to lend you a hand. They'll also be easier to manage than employees.
- Research locations - Permit costs change with locations. City centers might have lots of traffic but the costs might make them unviable. A lower foot traffic area with low permit expenses might make more sense. Do your research.
- Partner up - Buying in bulk always gets you discounts so why not buy ingredients with other food trucks? Both of you will be able to land discounts.
- Market - I'll detail marketing strategies in Chapter 6 but spend lots of time and effort on marketing. Customers will simply not hear you otherwise.
- DIY - Save startup costs by carrying out as many tasks as possible in the beginning. Painting the truck, setting up appliances, and decorating it, are tasks that you can do yourself. Don't sacrifice your brand image in the interests of saving costs but don't automatically hire outside help either.
- Research suppliers - Always compare prices. Every wholesaler has different prices, so take the time to research who has the best prices. Don't assume the first one offers the best price.
- Manage - Track your inventory and receipts. This is crucial for your success. Everything that is tracked can be improved.

Mistakes to Avoid

It's important to know what to do, but you need to be aware of what to avoid as well. Avoid the mistakes outlined below and you'll surely meet with success.

Ignoring Your Budget

The worst thing you can do is ignore your budget and base your spending on your feelings. Even worse, having no budget is something no business can recover from. Always outline your costs and stick to them. Remember that when you estimate costs, always estimate the worst-case scenario. This will help you view everything with a margin of safety built-in.

A margin of safety is a buffer that you can lean on during tough times. For example, if you budget inventory per month to be $4,000, but spend $3,000 instead, you'll feel as if you've saved $1,000. What's more, you'll have priced your menu according to the worst-case scenario. Every dollar less that you spend will result in greater profits for you. In essence, your plan and budget will have profits built into them.

Tracking your spending is important, so install a process that automatically ensures all of your receipts are logged and booked. Invest in a bookkeeping software and keep meticulous records. Keeping track of cash flow is more important for a business than its income. They're not the same. As I mentioned in the previous chapter, you don't have to deduct capital expenditures from income. If you earned a $1,000 profit in a month as earnings, this looks great. If you needed to spend $4,000 upgrading your truck, you've actually made a loss. The cash in your bank account always tells the truth, so track that rigorously.

Underestimating Costs

You will underestimate costs. This is natural if it's your first time running a business. What's not natural is continuously underestimating costs. Instead of assuming the worst-case scenario, you constantly assume the best-case scenario and end up doing yourself a lot of harm. It pays to be negative with regards to your cost projections. As I just explained, this builds a profit margin into your business automatically.

Most business owners aren't ready to face facts regarding their business. They want it to succeed so desperately that they fool themselves into thinking everything will be fine. Underestimating costs is a tell-tale sign of doing this.

Overestimating Profits

This is a cousin of the previous mistake. You must consider worst-case scenario costs and worst-case scenario profits. This means you should estimate costs to be on the higher side and revenues to be on the lower side. If your business can turn a profit under such harsh conditions, you'll mint money during good times. It's a great test of a business' resilience.

We tend to invest a lot of ourselves into our ideas, and it's easy to get emotional about your projects. It's great to be passionate. However, you shouldn't let passion get ahead of practicality. That's what creates losses.

Ignoring Marketing

Passion sometimes clouds our judgment with regards to marketing. We start thinking that the quality of our products are so obvious that people won't be able to help themselves and will flock to your business. In this day and age, this is incorrect. There are so many distractions out there that people have extremely short attention spans. Call it the effect of social media or whatever, but you need to remain as relevant to your users today, as you were yesterday.

This means occupying their mind space. The easiest way to do this is to stay at the top of their feeds and to generate publicity for yourself. You don't need to go viral all the time, but you should have a clear marketing plan. If you don't enjoy it, this is fine. However, don't just ignore it because you don't like it. That's not going to make you successful.

Hire someone to manage your social media feeds. There are many people and agencies who are willing to do this for you, so get in touch with them and negotiate a fee. Partner up with other food trucks and see if you can negotiate a bulk discount.

Paying Yourself Too Much

This is a common mistake that many new food truck owners make. You need to live and pay your bills, but this doesn't mean you pay yourself exorbitant amounts. You need to put money back into your business so that it can grow. Paying yourself every cent of profit you earn is going to take that much-needed capital away from the business.

Besides, if you have an investor onboard, it's not going to look good to them. They've sunk money into your business only for you to pay yourself large amounts. This increases the time they need to wait to see their money come back to them.

Chapter 4:

Finding the Right Truck

Your truck is your place of business and it holds the key to your success. You'll need to find the right truck, make sure it's within your budget, and then customize it to suit your needs. You can buy the best-looking truck, but if it cannot accommodate your cooking needs, then it's of no use. Customization can cost you a lot of money and this adds to your startup costs.

This is over and above the money you pay to buy your truck. In short, your truck easily eats up the greatest amount of your startup capital. Being judicious with your choices is extremely important. Before you even think about buying a truck, visit your local county's or city's office and ask to meet the official who is in charge of food truck design safety reviews. Have them give you a printed leaflet of all the regulations and safety requirements. You don't need to use them just yet, but once you've bought your truck, you'll need to customize it and these regulations will help you avoid many headaches.

Buying a Truck

As I mentioned in the previous chapter, you can expect to pay between $50,000 to $150,000 for a food truck. This price range covers used and new trucks of all sizes. It might be tempting to minimize costs and opt for the cheapest truck you can find. This isn't always a good option. Your truck is where you'll be conducting business so you need to balance costs with usability. The last thing you want is for your truck to break down or cost you a pile in maintenance.

New trucks are the most reliable and have the "shine" factor going for them. They'll also depreciate like a rock thrown in a lake. Depreciation refers to the decrease in value. While they might be mobile restaurants, they're still vehicles that are going to experience wear and tear. Unlike normal vehicles, they can't be used by just about anybody. Other food truck owners are the only ones who'll be interested in them. This means depreciation is a huge hit.

On the flip side, you can reasonably expect to hang onto a truck for a long time if your business does well. The longer you can hang onto it, the less you need to worry about depreciation. This is because even a used truck will depreciate to zero on a long enough timeline. If you've never run a business before, it's best to opt for a used truck. There are many challenges you'll face and it's best to minimize your costs. If you've run a business previously, whether in the food industry or not, you can consider a new truck. You'll have a better idea of how cash flow works so it's worth taking the risk.

If you're a first-time business owner, consider renting a truck. This isn't the most optimal financial decision but it reduces your upfront costs massively. It places a cash flow burden on your business though, so you'll need to account for an additional cost. Here's what the decision of buying versus renting boils down to. If you buy a truck using a loan, you'll pay monthly interest payments. How do those interest payments compare to rental costs? Choose the lower option.

If you're buying a truck for cash (without a loan), the choice is a bit more complex. Where could you have invested that cash and how much cash flow would that investment have generated? Let's say you decide to pay $2,000 per month renting a truck, and invest the $80,000 it would have cost to buy it into marketing. Will the buzz generated by that additional $80,000 lead to at least $2,000 in sales per month? If your average purchase price is $10, this is 200 additional sales per month or seven more sales per day.

From a common-sense perspective, changing your location to high traffic one can bring in an additional seven sales per day. It isn't a huge number to hit. In this case, you'd be better off buying the truck since you can eliminate the $2,000 monthly payment and switch locations to generate seven additional sales per day. Weigh all options before choosing which one to go with.

Your psyche also plays an important role. Some people are more comfortable renting their premises than buying it. It makes projecting cash flow easier, and it's easier to switch strategies. If your current choice of cuisine isn't working, you can simply rent another truck instead of having to repurpose your existing one.

Perhaps a middle of the road solution might suit first time owners best. Rent a truck for the first two to three months so that you have a good handle on cash flow. Buy a truck after that depending on how well your business is doing. If it's doing well, buying the truck will boost your cash flow per month and your business will gain an asset.

Lowering Costs

Trailers are a great option if you're short of cash. They're smaller than trucks and cost anywhere from $15,000 to $50,000. A trailer costs less but there are some additional costs you'll have to account for. For starters, you'll need to pay parking costs for the trailer as well as your vehicle. The trailer will be less mobile since you'll have to hitch it to your vehicle to tow it everywhere. Lastly, if you don't have a vehicle that can tow a trailer, that's an additional expense. If this is the case, you might as well invest in a food truck purchase.

As ideal as it sounds, it's hard to rent trailers. You might find a deal through the classifieds, or you could rent one from another owner who doesn't have immediate use for it. These deals are hard to come by so it's best to not rely on them. Trailers also tend to be smaller in size than food trucks so you'll have to make some compromises. Will these compromises cause you to serve less food? You'll have to take this into account.

While the costs of starting this business are high, it pays to view these startup costs as an investment. You're not going to get your money back within a day but you'll be creating an asset that pays you money steadily over time. Most first time business owners think of their startup costs versus monthly profits in terms of a breakeven calculation. For example, if you invested $80,000 upfront and make $1,000 profits every month, it'll take you 80 months to recover your money.

This is an incorrect business calculation. By investing $80,000 you're creating an asset that can be sold for some price down the road. If you can sell your used food truck for $50,000, your real investment is $30,000 (80000-50000.) At $1,000 per month you'll recover this money in 30 months. If you're paying yourself a salary of $4,000 every month, your true earnings from the business are $5,000 per month. Your recovery time is now a mere six months.

Besides, if you're planning on owning the truck for a long time, does it really matter how much you spend on it upfront? As long as you have the cash to finance the purchase, it doesn't matter. You need to focus on creating the best asset possible. For example, you could buy a new ice cream truck for $150,000, but if you're serving Mexican food, this is a liability. Instead, a used truck of $70,000 is a better investment. However, if that $70,000 truck doesn't give you enough space to cook great food and serve customers, it's not a great asset. A $90,000 truck might be better.

If this $90,000 truck allows you to cook great food easily, drive quickly and reliably to locations and doesn't bleed you dry in maintenance, it's a wonderful asset. You'll make more money from it as compared to the $70,000 truck. You'll spend more, but you'll make more. Think of your truck purchase in these terms. I'm not saying expensive is better. Far from it.

The quality of your investment depends on the asset you create. Don't think of it in terms of how much it costs. Instead, look at how much money it can make you and how easily it can do this. Match its price to how much money you have and make an appropriate decision. What if the $90,000 truck is ideal but you can only afford the $70,000 one? It's likely you'll find yourself in this situation. If this happens you have a few choices.

First, can you buy a trailer that is as big as the $90,000 truck? If you have an existing towing vehicle, a trailer is the perfect choice for you. If you don't have a vehicle, and you can't strike any bargains for trucks like the $90,000 one, consider renting a truck like it for a few months. Keep the $70,000 or a large part of it in an interest-bearing account and add your monthly profits to this account. Once it builds up to $90,000, buy the truck. Alternatively, save until you have enough to finance a down-payment on the $90,000 truck and buy it using a loan.

Don't ever compromise and buy an inferior asset because it's cheaper. If a $70,000 truck doesn't make you money, you're not "saving" money. In fact, it's costing you money. Many first-time business owners make this mistake. You have to think in terms of assets, not expenses. Anything expenditure that makes your business a better asset and produces money for you is a worthwhile investment, as long as you can afford it. If you can't afford it, build your savings until you can.

Choosing a Truck

How will you know which truck is right for you? There are certain factors you can evaluate when buying one. The most obvious factor is the style of food you'll be serving. Some trucks come equipped with appliances, while many don't. If you're buying a used truck that has appliances, don't pay a premium for them. Used appliances sell for less than 10% of their purchase price. If the seller is using this to justify their asking price, don't fall for it. You can buy used appliances separately and install them yourself.

Your type of cuisine determines the amount of space you'll need. If you're cooking pizzas in a truck, you'll need more space for an industrial oven and for dough preparation. If you're grilling burgers, you won't need as much space since a hot grill is more than enough for your needs. If you're serving a range of soups as found in Asian cuisine, you'll need even less space. Visualize what you want your cooking space to look like and evaluate trucks accordingly.

The type of food you'll be making also dictates whether you'll be using a commercial kitchen to prepare food or not. An Asian soup-based menu doesn't require much onsite cooking. However, you will need a kitchen to prepare everything beforehand. If this is your cuisine, you can opt for a cheap trailer and invest more of your money into commercial kitchen space. The need for a commercial kitchen should be balanced with your truck's costs. If you can spend more to buy a bigger truck that allows you to cook everything in it, you can save on monthly expenses that a commercial kitchen will create.

Having said that, most food truck operators need a commercial space to create good food. Once again, you need to think in terms of assets instead of defaulting to an expense-based thought process. This directly impacts your cost considerations, as I discussed previously. Before choosing a truck, it pays to examine your proposed locations as well. A bigger truck might not be able to navigate smaller locations.

As a rule of thumb, the bigger your truck is, the smaller the number of locations that will suit it. A smaller truck can get into more places, but if it's too small, you won't be able to cook any good food in it. Balance is what you need to aim for. Your customer personas also play into your choice of truck. They'll have certain expectations of your business, and if they find it visually unappealing, your food's taste won't matter as much. Customers will come to you if you cook great food, but it's going to be harder to attract them if your truck doesn't look good, or look like what it's supposed to.

For example, if you're serving pizzas from an impossibly small truck, customers might assume you're reheating frozen pizzas and their perception of your business drops. The style of your truck also matters. Many food truck owners customize the appearance of their truck with appendages to make them stand out. Is your truck suitable for this? If it can't accommodate certain design additions, then it's not a good investment.

How much traffic do you expect every day and how many employees will you have? This ties into your space demands. A food truck that serves a large number of customers requires more storage space for ingredients and other items relevant to the food you're cooking. Such a business will also need to have at least one other employee cooking food.

Most food trucks require at least two people serving customers. One to organize the order tickets, bill customers, and deliver food, and another to cook food and manage ingredient levels. A third person might be needed to attract customers to a truck and to manage lines. If lines get too long, it's a good idea to keep customers occupied by giving them a drink and collecting money for it before they order their food.

Locating Dealers

Once you have a good idea of what sort of truck you'd like, it's time to find dealers. The riskiest way to source a truck seller is to look at sites like eBay and Craigslist. You'll land great deals, but they're risky. You don't know what the truck has been used for previously and in some areas, you run the risk of buying a former drug lab.

It's best to stick to reputed sellers. Prestige Food Trucks, Cruising Kitchens, and Foodtrucks.net are examples of manufacturers who list new and used food trucks. The first two are custom manufacturers so you'll be able to buy just new trucks from them. The third source lists a variety of trucks and buses on offer and some of them are used. Buying from these reputed manufacturers might cost more but it'll save you a ton of headaches. You'll also be able to use their guidance when it comes to compliance needs. For example, most local governments require trucks to have a three sink washing arrangement. Custom manufacturers can inform you of what the regulations are and create appropriate designs for you.

Food Truck Empire is a website that lists all dealers by state. You can narrow your search down to your zip code and contact dealers. You'll be more likely to find used food trucks by employing this method. When dealing with truck dealers, you'll need to summon all of your negotiation skills. These dealers are used to selling to business owners and their skills are more sophisticated than your average used-car salesperson. However, you'll find good deals on trucks by approaching a dealer close to you.

A way of figuring out good prices for trucks is to approach existing food truck operators and ask them where they bought their trucks. Also ask them how well their truck runs and who they recommend. You'll get some great tips about what to watch out for when buying a truck. Who knows, they might even be willing to sell their truck to you.

Customization

Buying a truck is just the first step. You need to customize it to suit your needs and this presents its own challenges. If you've filled the steps listed thus far, you'll have a good idea of everything that you need. At the very least, you should have your menu designed by this point. Prepare a list of everything you'll need to store in the truck. What does your cooking process look like? Which food will you store in the truck, which ones will you cook, and what will you need to cook this food? Listing food storage needs and preparation methods in detail is helpful to the design process.

It'll also help you choose the right equipment. Make it a point to also include all future menu items that you can think of. This will help you prepare in advance and you won't run into costly design changes down the road.

List Your Equipment

It's now time to tackle all the equipment you'll need in your kitchen. Create a detailed list along with the specifications. Broadly speaking, all food equipment falls into three categories. These are food prep, storage, and cooking. At the very least, most food trucks will need a grill or a cooking surface, refrigeration, and food warmers (hot plates.) Your individual needs will vary depending on how you choose to run operations.

Keep in mind that you can't remove your household stove top and bolt it into the truck. Commercial food equipment has to meet safety standards. It's a good idea to speak to an owner of a food truck, or the seller of the truck, to understand what these need to be. If you're purchasing a new truck from a manufacturer, they'll take care of everything for you.

In the case of a used truck, the equipment it has should already conform to commercial codes. However, if you're planning on installing your own equipment you'll need to look at these regulations again. Measure the cooking space in your kitchen and also note any service windows, doorways and electrical outlets. Take a lot of photos of the space and note all measurements. For new trucks, it's best to create a detailed engineering drawing and present this to the manufacturer.

You can create a rough sketch of what you want, and hire a freelancer on a website such as Fiverr or Upwork to create a 2D and 3D rendering of your design. Some manufacturers also have in-house design and mock-up services that you can use. It'll cost you money, but this is bundled together with the cost of a new truck. Take a note of the existing flooring material and air vents.

These are extremely important. The interior of your truck is going to be hot and the last thing you want is a flammable surface close to you. Make a note of exhaust vents as well. In the case of a used truck, you'll want to make sure everything works as advertised. If you're buying a truck from a dealer, they'll typically provide you with the maintenance history and working condition report. If buying from an individual seller, it pays to hire a mechanic and an electrician. These people can check the condition of the vehicle as well as the state of the appliances.

Water and Power

Your equipment dictates your water and power needs. You can't plug your appliances into an outlet so you'll need an external source of power, like a generator. You'll also need to account for water storage, propane tanks, and other energy storage mechanisms. An electrician will help you figure this out and will recommend installations for you. Don't try to DIY this portion of your truck. It's crucial that electrical and water systems run well so that you can run your business smoothly.

The biggest maintenance headaches come from the wiring and plumbing within your truck. The vehicle itself will be driven to and fro between locations so it doesn't experience as much wear and tear as a regular vehicle would. You won't have many engine or oil problems. It's the kitchen that will need regular maintenance. So make sure everything within it works well right from the start. If your kitchen goes down, so does your business.

Exterior Considerations

While the interior is all about efficiency, your exterior is all about attracting customers to your truck. What sort of appendages will you need to ensure your customers are well served and that they find your truck appealing? For example, many trucks attach a counter to the outside of the truck for condiments and napkins. Customers can help themselves without disrupting the inside of the truck.

There are some external additions you need to consider. For example, a security awning makes a lot of sense. These awnings slide over the exterior of your truck and protect the doors, windows, and anything else you might have attached to the outside of your truck. They'll prevent vandalism and other damage that might occur when you leave your truck parked overnight.

A retractable awning gives your order window a more intimate feel. By extending upwards, it provides your customers with shelter. A bonus of such an awning is that you'll be able to hear their orders more clearly since sound is contained in the area. These awnings will also come in handy when it rains or snows. Customers will always flock to a truck that has an awning in such conditions versus one that doesn't.

External TV panels might seem excessively fancy, but they're actually very easy to install. Some food trucks prefer to bolt chalkboards to the outside and use these to display their menus. Every day, owners write menu items onto the board using chalk and, if you're someone who can create intricate designs using chalk, it's worth it. However, if you're like most people, all you'll do is get your hands dirty.

A TV panel can be used to display all of your menu items and you can even include graphics in it. An LCD panel doesn't cost much these days, and they're completely programmable. Just make sure you have a backup to display your menu in case the electronics fail or if it starts raining. Some trucks encase them within the body so the screen is protected while others simply bolt a TV to the outside. They'll draw more power from your truck but if they're attractive, it'll draw customers in.

Speakers are also helpful. Playing music through them or making announcements via speakers builds a greater sense of community among your customers. It'll certainly keep them entertained while they wait in line. Another appendage that helps customers remain comfortable is a misting system. This is especially true in hot areas. Your customers will appreciate it. It'll place a strain on your water system but it's a worthwhile investment.

You will need service windows, needless to say. The size of these windows can be changed depending on your needs. Larger service windows always work better than smaller ones. They also double as great ventilation sources. A benefit of large ventilation windows is that your customers will be able to smell the food you're cooking and this will provide an additional attraction. You don't want to make your service window so large that it becomes unwieldy. There should be clear signs that indicate where your customers can order and where they can pick up their food.

A huge part of your exterior is your vinyl wrap. This ties in with your marketing strategy and I'll discuss this in detail in Chapter 6. However, an exterior wrap can help you stand out even more. As long as it doesn't interfere with the rest of your truck's workings, it's a good choice.

Approving the Final Design

Now comes the tough bit. All of your plans need to be translated to engineering drawings that clearly indicate the dimensions of your kitchen and your exteriors. You'll also need to create blueprints that indicate your plumbing systems and fire safety equipment. You can hire a freelancer to do this for you or you can use the services of a manufacturer.

The manufacturer will have both the ability to create drawings as well as knowledge of the latest health and safety regulations. You don't have to worry about your design being rejected. However, they do cost money and you'll have to buy a new truck. You can check with existing food truck owners for recommendations for designers. There are design-only firms that can provide you with all the technical drawings you need, but it can be hard to find them for a first-time buyer.

Once your drawings are complete, you'll need to have them reviewed by your local authority. Check with your local county office for the official who is in charge of reviewing food truck safety designs and schedule an appointment with them. If everything is good, they'll approve your design and you'll need to implement it. Keep in mind that even used food trucks need to receive approval irrespective of whether they were approved for use in the past or not.

If there are changes needed, you'll need to remodel your design. It can take you a few tries to get it all right if you're doing it yourself. So be patient and take your time with it. Always keep the health and safety of you, your employees, and your customers at the forefront of your mind. This helps reduce any reviews down the road.

The food truck purchase and design process is an intricate one. It's much easier if you opt to work with a manufacturer with prior experience, but the trade-off is that you'll pay higher prices. If you buy a used vehicle, you'll have to figure out many things by yourself but you'll pay lower prices. It's up to you to decide what works best. Choose to utilize your time wisely and keep budget constraints in mind at all times. You want to save money but don't end up being penny-wise but pound foolish. Once your truck is bought and designed, it's time to dive deep into the world of permits and licensing.

Chapter 5:

How to Stay on the Right Side of

the Law

As a food truck owner you're going to be subjected to a ton of regulations and laws. It'll seem as if there are a mountain of laws you need to comply with, and it's going to be tempting for you to quit in the face of this. However, I urge you to not lose heart. Regulations and laws are difficult to comprehend at first, but this is because most of us try to take them in all at once. Instead, break them down into smaller pieces and process them one by one.

There are two broad sets of regulations you need to follow: Federal and State. Federal regulations are pretty light and will become onerous only if you serve alcohol or tobacco from your truck. Your federal requirements boil down to two things as you'll see in this chapter. State laws are a much bigger concern and are far more relevant to you. The troublesome aspect is that these local laws can be difficult to research. Many states still live in the dark ages and have outdated websites.

While research can be tough if you live in such a state, it's far from impossible. Before you begin, set aside at least a month to research all the laws you need to comply with. Ideally, you'll do this before you even write your business plan. The good news is that once you understand these laws, you won't need to worry about learning them all over again. They'll become second nature to you and you'll manage to comply with them easily.

It's best to take even two months to research the topic. There are four broad topics that all licenses and regulations fall into. These are:

- Local licensing requirements
- Health code standards
- Commissary requirements
- Parking laws

It's going to take you a lot of time and run-ins with bureaucracy to figure out all of these laws, so it's best to prepare yourself for frustration. That way, if you manage to find something easily, it'll come as a nice surprise. It helps to start with federal requirements. All you need to do is form a company and get yourself an EIN or Employer Identification Number.

There are four types of corporate structures you can choose from. These are; sole-proprietorship, limited liability company (LLC), C-corporation, and S-corporation. Many food truckers begin as sole proprietorships since this costs literally nothing. If you sell anything without a trade license, you're working as a sole-proprietor. However, this is a very risky business structure for a food truck owner.

If one of your customers falls sick or if one of your employees suffers an injury at work, your personal assets will be on the line when they claim damages. By incorporating your business, you'll build a barrier between such claims and your assets. You don't want to lose your house because someone had an allergic reaction to your food.

The structure that makes the most sense is an LLC. This structure allows you to limit your liability to just the company's assets. It also allows you to pass through all earnings to yourself so you pay tax on your earnings just once. This is in contrast to the corporation (C and S) structures where you'll pay taxes twice, once at the company level and once at the personal level, on any salary you pay yourself.

The key to making an LLC work well for you is to establish a separate business account for your company and spend everything related to your business from there. Pay for your vehicle from that account and not from your personal account. If you don't separate your accounts, a judge might rule that there isn't enough separation to justify a limited liability status if someone brings a claim against you.

Establishing an LLC is as simple as filing online or approaching a lawyer. You can use a site like LegalZoom to do this easily. Costs usually run up to a few hundreds of dollars before service fees. Your lawyer or service will also act as your company's registered agent and for a fee, will take care of the filings you need to make every year. Alternatively, you can give this task to your accountant.

The next step is to file for an EIN. This number will be used when you file your taxes. If you're not hiring employees, you can file taxes using your SSN. You can have your accountant apply for your EIN, or you can call the IRS yourself and have one assigned to you. Your EIN will usually be activated within 30 days after it's issued. You can open a bank account without an EIN or with one that has been issued but isn't yet active.

That takes care of your federal obligations. You'll need to file taxes by the end of January for the previous calendar year, and you'll then file your personal taxes in April. Since taxes are passed through, you'll pay the LLC's taxes in January and the remainder of your income taxes in April. It's crucial that you keep meticulous records and track all of your receipts. Your accountant will prepare a profit and loss statement at the end of the year but you can create interim ones using software such as

Quickbooks or Zoho. Now that your federal obligations are done, let's move on to the local ones.

Challenges You'll Face

It might feel as if you're headed to battle at times when trying to figure out local laws. Here are a few tips to keep in mind when you deal with these issues. They'll help you remain sane through tough times.

Assume There are no Laws

There are still some municipalities and counties that don't have food truck laws in place. Despite the business model having been around forever, government officials aren't always up to speed on how the business works. You must prepare yourself to explain what a food truck is over and over to different people. You'll likely meet with people who have no clue about restaurant licensing needs, and you might even end up talking to someone who is in charge of taxi regulation.

Remain calm throughout all of this and eventually, you'll find someone who can let you know what the laws are or whether they even exist. If your county doesn't have laws you can assume that usual restaurant licensing needs apply to you and you can serve food out of a truck. This is good news for you. However, laws can always be created down the road so design your truck in accordance with laws from other jurisdictions.

This way, if the county does decide to wake up and introduce laws, you're not going to be caught out by them.

Be Prepared for Restrictive Laws

The biggest advantage of a food truck is that you can park it wherever you want and start serving food. Right? Wrong! Many jurisdictions have strict requirements surrounding where a food truck can ply its services. In places such as Boston, a food truck cannot park within a certain distance of a restaurant and it can only remain parked in an area for a certain number of hours a day. In other places, food trucks cannot operate outside of designated zones.

The lesson here is to treat your food truck as a business. It's not a mobile version of your kitchen at home where you can roll up and start serving food. There are a number of hoops to jump through when you get started, so pay attention to all of them. Pay special attention to the size and specifications the government requires of trucks. This impacts your bottom line directly.

Some governments limit the size of your truck, which means you can't serve anything out of a truck and will be restricted to a trailer. Other cities will require you to serve food out of a minimum sized area which means trailers will be disqualified. Laws can get intricate and local government officials couldn't care less about your business. Stay strong and keep digging. This is precisely why you need at least a month or two months to figure out all of this stuff.

Categorize Your Information

There is a lot of information you need to gather so it's a good idea to categorize all of it. Here are the main categories you'll need to gather information about:

- Which licenses you'll need - You'll need a license for the truck, a special driver's license, and a business license at the very least. You'll need local business permits but in some areas, you might even need state and county permits.
- Where can you park? - Which locations can you park, what are the zoning requirements, can you park at metered locations, how long can you park, and so on.
- Truck specifications - Does the city specify truck dimensions? Make a thorough note of these.
- Health and safety - You'll need detailed specifications on preparing food, storing it, serving it, your employees' work

areas, water access, waste disposal, bathroom requirements (for your customers to access), and fire handling systems. This is a huge area and can be subdivided into its own sections depending on the complexity of local regulations.

- Where you apply - Which office handles permit applications and is there a cap? Many areas have a waiting list and limit the number of food truck permits that are issued.
- Insurance - What kind of insurance you will need and what are the coverage limits?

Sources of Information

As you can see, there's a lot of information you need to gather before you can get going. Where can you find all this information, though? Here's a handy list of places that will have everything you need:

1. Local government offices - The local chamber of commerce, small business administration department, and the health department are the usual suspects. If food trucks are popular in your area, they might have all the information you need online. You can call or email the office to ask questions. If food trucks are close to nonexistent in your area, then be prepared to hoof it down to the local office.

2. Food truck associations - These will be a lifesaver for you. Existing food truck owners usually band together to form associations that help new owners get started. Often, they'll compile a list of answers to the most commonly asked questions for you to peruse. You can find listings by searching online or by asking an existing food truck owner if an organization exists. Another advantage of an association is that you can network with other owners and learn more information about the business.

3. Websites - Websites, such as FoodTruckr, are a great resource for food truck owners. In addition to this, you can also check the SBA website to read about the laws that govern your

locality. Subscribe to news alerts on Google and you'll be able to stay up to speed with all the changes taking place.

Organize Yourself

Given the volume of information you'll be gathering, it's best to get organized. This way you won't have to deal with information overload and can easily retrieve whatever you need quickly. Here are some tips to help you get organized and take bite-sized pieces out of the information you need to collect (*How to Start a Food Truck 19: Organize Your Licenses and Permits*, 2020)/:

- Make a checklist - The best way to track everything you need to research is to make a checklist. Leave some room for additional items since they'll crop up during your research.
- Schedule time - Whether you're taking a few hours every day or getting everything done over a weekend, schedule some time for getting all of this done and stick to your schedule. Don't get distracted or postpone your plans.
- Keep records - Whether you're communicating via email, phone, or in person, record everything. If you're uncomfortable recording someone in-person, ask them to give everything to you in writing. This way you'll know for sure whether the information you're collecting and your interpretation of it is correct. It'll also help you back your claims up if you should be questioned about potential violations.
- Store - Organize your document storage. Keep everything in one place. A practice that really helps is to scan all the documents you collect and store them in a single folder. This ensures you have backups in case you lose the physical copies. Keep records of everything, including; meeting times, information discussed and the contact person's relevant information (name, title, office, contact number, and email.)
- Consistency - You're dealing with the government, and they're sticklers for consistency. When filling out forms, keep

everything the same. Don't use a nickname in one form and your formal name in another. This sort of thing drives bureaucrats mad, so you'll only create obstacles for yourself. Stay consistent with the information you provide. The same advice applies to when you're describing your business as well. Rehearse a few lines in advance and repeat that whenever someone asks you about it. Minimize their chances of getting confused.

Permits You'll Need

Now that you know all of the challenges you'll face, how you need to get organized, and where you need to go to collect all this information and apply for your permits, it's time to look at the permits themselves. Every jurisdiction requires different permits, so make sure you check with your local government office. At a minimum you'll need to have your business incorporated as well as an EIN if you're employing people. Note: You don't need to have incorporated your business during the information collection stage, but it needs to be done before you apply for permits.

Tax Registration and Business License

These are federal and state requirements as I explained earlier. They're straightforward to apply for. Make sure you open your business bank account after you receive the license from your local government. Most governments deliver this online, along with your articles of incorporation and other relevant documents. Store them safely. Deposit cash into that account and start spending money from that account for all expenses related to the business.

Aside from your general business license, you'll also need state specific licenses if you're operating a food truck. Check with your local government's office to figure out what these licenses are.

Local Permits

Your local government's office is also where you'll apply for local permits. You'll need several of these, make no mistake. Each of the licenses mentioned below has different requirements so you'll need to check with the authorities as to how they work. The list below is not exhaustive but it's what you'll need at a minimum:

- Alarm permit
- Local tax permit
- Signage permit
- Local zoning permit
- Health and food safety permit

You can typically apply for all of these permits from the same office at once. If applying for all of these permits is too much for you, you can use the services of an attorney or a professional who can help you with this.

DBA

DBA stands for "Doing Business As" and it's the brand name of your truck. Your business can be incorporated with a boring XYZ Foods LLC moniker, but you can do business as Macho Nacho Food Truck. You can file your DBA with the local government and it's a straightforward filing in most jurisdictions.

Employer Requirements

This is a big one. If you're planning on hiring employees, you'll need an EIN as I mentioned earlier. It's best to seek the help of an accountant or attorney during this phase. There are many obligations you'll have as an employer, such as social security contributions and your tax obligations also change. Going over all of them is beyond the scope of this book. Make sure your accountant explains everything to you, especially with regards to insurance and deductions you can take.

When you hire employees, you'll need them to fill out Form I-9. This form verifies whether that person can legally work in the US. You'll then head over to the e-verify website at www.everify.gov and enter their information. The form will be processed and you'll be notified of the result in a few working days. Once verified, you'll have them fill out Form W-4, which lists the withholding amount. This is the money you'll withhold from their paycheck for taxes and pay to the government.

Once you hire an employee, you'll have to report this to the state government within 20 calendar days. Check with the local government's office about reporting requirements. Most states allow you to do this online.

Posters

If you've ever been in a commercial kitchen, you'll have noticed the "employees must wash hands" signage. This is a government requirement. You'll also need to post notices informing your employees of the health and safety regulations, as well as their rights in the workplace. These notices will also contain information about the minimum wage and worker's compensation.

Miscellaneous

There are a bunch of other requirements you need to follow that aren't necessarily covered by a permit. Prominent among these is the presence of a bathroom or toilet for your customer. Obviously, you can't build one into your truck, so you'll need to park near a public facility. The commissary kitchens you use also come under the purview of the government and you can expect surprise inspections of your space.

Traditionally, places of business are inspected once a year but surprise inspections are possible. Make sure to check with the local food truck association and other operators in the area for any requirements that you might miss. There will always be subtleties that you'll miss, especially with regards to the way your truck ought to be designed.

It might seem like governments don't want people to start businesses, and their employees' behavior does nothing to change this perception. Believe it or not, local governments want people opening businesses and bringing cash into the community. All of these permits are put in place to ensure your customers are safeguarded and that they're not inconvenienced. Prepare for the worst and you'll have a good experience of it.

Insurance

There's a major requirement I've purposely left out because it deserves its own section. This is insurance. Any business requires robust insurance coverage and a food truck business is no different. In fact, food trucks face additional claims that traditional restaurants don't and this means they need better coverage. Shop for insurance deals with various providers and work with the ones who know the requirements of the mobile food business.

Once you get in touch with a representative, explain all facets of your business to them, including how you plan on serving your customers. Insurance companies offer policies that are suited to restaurants and then change a few terms here and there to suit your needs. This is standard practice in the industry, so don't be alarmed by it. You have additional needs though so you'll need to ask some questions pertinent to you.

Questions to Ask

You're not just a restaurant, you're a vehicle as well. With this in mind inquire whether you'll be covered in case of an auto accident. What if someone on a bicycle crashes into your truck while it's stationary and breaks a headlamp? Will you be covered for damage from uninsured patrons? Your truck is technically your place of business and anyone who injures themselves on your premises can sue you. Will you be sued in this scenario? If you are, does insurance cover it?

The most important item to check is whether your insurance covers a mobile business. You'd think this is obvious but it sometimes slips by unattended. What happens if your truck is stolen or vandalized? To prevent such claims from occurring, insurers will require you to park your truck in a secure facility. As I mentioned earlier, you can't park your truck on the street. Local ordinances prohibit parking RVs and other commercial vehicles in street parking spaces. Even if you can park them in your driveway, how long will it be before your truck is vandalized or stolen?

You have a range of choices when it comes to parking. You can park it in a roofed warehouse where your truck will be stored inside away from the elements. This is the safest option but it's also the most expensive. You can opt for semi-covered parking. Your truck will be outside but it'll have a roof over it. These premises are still pretty secure and are usually a part of a larger, fully covered warehouse facility. One step down the ladder is uncovered outdoor parking. You'll simply park your truck in a lot with other vehicles. Needless to say, these locations are not the safest and there's no guarantee that your vehicle won't be broken into. The location of the parking yard is important, so make sure you evaluate this thoroughly.

An unconventional choice is to park it in existing commercial lots. Businesses such as RV sales lots and large warehouse suppliers have parking space in their premises and might agree to let you park your vehicle for a fee. They won't advertise so you'll need to ask them about it. Just make sure this arrangement is covered by insurance. Unfortunately, insurers usually decline these facilities.

Other unconventional parking solutions include approaching gas stations that are popular with truckers. These facilities are used to having truckers camp overnight on their premises, so in exchange for buying some food and drinks from the store, you can score free parking. An increasingly popular option is Walmart. A lot depends on the location. Some Walmarts allow overnight parking while others have RVs and other vehicles towed away. Check with your local store first. Lastly, if you know of any casinos nearby, check with them.

You don't have to gamble your money, you could simply buy food and drinks from their restaurant every night. In exchange, you could score free parking or parking for a small fee, and know that your truck is secure. After all, casinos have high security oversight and are used to monitoring people milling about. Check with your insurance provider whether any of these nontraditional options are covered or not.

If you're buying a trailer, you'll need special insurance for this. You'll also need to check with your vehicle's insurer whether your policy covers damages when driving for business purposes. You might have to get yourself a new policy. Lastly, check if your policy covers you for food poisoning claims. You don't want to poison your customers but who knows what might happen?

Typical Coverage

A policy for a mobile food vendor usually includes a few terms. Here they are in no order of importance (*Buy the Insurance You Need for Your Food Truck Business*, 2020):

- Commercial auto liability - This covers all vehicles used in business operations. Be careful of personal auto-insurance policies that cover business usage. These will not suit your needs. First, a food truck is not a personal vehicle. Second, the insurance limits of those personal policies will not be enough to cover damages if your truck has many appendages so get a commercial policy.
- General liability - This is a catch-all coverage that takes care of everything that isn't addressed by your other coverages. For example, what protects you when you're opening your business during the day and someone runs into your parked truck. This is where general liability comes into the picture. Discuss every aspect of your business with your insurance provider, and they'll choose the right features for you.
- Business personal property- Business, personal, what? This policy seems nonsensical but it covers all appendages to your truck that are not a permanent part of it. For example, if you hitch a smoker to the back of your truck, this policy covers it.
- Worker's compensation- If any of your employees are injured on the job, this policy covers their medical bills.
- Unemployment insurance - This policy pays your former employees until they find new work.
- Umbrella liability - Despite the name, this coverage has nothing to do with umbrellas. It's additional protection over and above your other protection limits. For example, if all of your limits add up to $5 million but you get sued for $6 million, umbrella liability will cover the additional million.

When you check for insurance policies with a provider, they'll need a list of drivers. These drivers' records will be checked and if one of them happens to have a poor record, you can expect coverage to be pulled. You'll have to either withdraw that person from the list of drivers or pay a huge amount to cover them as well. To avoid headaches, you can check each driver's motor vehicle report or MVR with the local DMV (another jewel of local government!)

Here are the red flags to watch out for. If in the past 36 months, if a driver has more than the specified number of incidents as mentioned below, they're likely to not be approved(*Buy the Insurance You Need for Your Food Truck Business*, 2020):

- One moving violation and two accidents
- Two moving violations and one accident
- Three moving violations

No one should have any serious moving violations such as a DUI, auto felony conviction, or a suspended license.

Additional Insured Certificates

Here's an insider's tip. When you attend events and festivals, the organizers will ask you to add them as "additional insured" parties on your policy. What does this mean? This term refers to entities outside of yourself that are covered by your policy. For example, if someone suffers food poisoning from your food at an event, the event organizer is liable to be sued for damages. Having them as an additional insured on your policy protects them.

The catch is that these certificates cost money. An insurance firm can charge $50 and above for each certificate. If you attend five events every month, that's a significant cost. Insurance providers who are unfamiliar with mobile food business requirements often neglect this coverage and might even be unaware of it. They'll charge you an arm and a leg for these certificates. Try to get your insurer to issue you unlimited additional insured certificates in exchange for a bump in the premium.

If you pay $500 extra as premiums for unlimited certificates, you can attend all the events you want. Even better, see if you can get them to offer the certificates to you for free. Get it in writing from them so that there is no confusion down the road.

Chapter 6:

Marketing 101 - Making Your Food Truck a Success Right From the Get-Go

Your marketing plan is technically a section of your overall business plan but these days, it's perhaps the most essential part of your business. Without marketing, you're not going to go anywhere. Consumers have far too many options these days to frequent spots that don't work to grab their attention. The flip side is that spreading word of mouth reviews is now easier than ever thanks to social media. Who knows? With the right ingredients, you might find yourself going viral.

Let's start with the basics. What is a marketing plan? Think of it as a business plan for your marketing. Just as how you'll refer to your business plan to keep tabs on yourself and use it as a reference document during tough times, your marketing plan functions the same way for your marketing efforts. In fact, your marketing plan is a more fluid document that will change a lot at first, and then more gradually as you zero in on the marketing strategies that work for you.

Your plan should serve as an instruction manual for all of your marketing efforts. Leave nothing up in the air. Detail everything meticulously. An important detail to document are your metrics. Every digital marketing outlet these days has a means of measuring your return on ad spend. With paid ads, it's very obviously displayed on ad dashboards. With organic methods, such as an Instagram account, metrics are more circuitous. You can track follower counts, new followers gained, and the number of people who tagged you, for example.

These metrics will help you figure out whether you're reaching your goals for customer growth and retention. Retention is an area that not enough business owners focus on. A returning customer is worth twice as much as a new one. This is why incentives such as a loyalty card are so powerful. They keep people coming back to you for more, and as your retained customers grow, they spread the word about you for free, leading to more new customers.

Your marketing plan will outline the strategies you'll use to promote new customer acquisition and growth. It'll also outline who will be in charge of these activities. What your budget will be and so on. Your marketing plan should complement your business plan. Indeed, you'll refer to your business plan quite a lot when you create your marketing plan.

Before we get into the details of drawing up a marketing plan, I want to caution you against dismissing marketing elements as corporate or management consultant mumbo-jumbo. It's true that some of the jargon can get needlessly complicated and markets like to coin ridiculous sounding terms, but they're important for your business. Marketing has evolved dramatically over the past decade and it's important for you to remain up to speed with it.

So pay attention to all the points in this chapter. They'll ensure your business will be successful before you even launch it.

Preliminary Work

Before you begin crafting your marketing plan, you need some input. An effective plan needs two analyses to be conducted. These will give you a well-rounded picture of what you need to do. The two analyses are:

1. Competitor analysis

2. SWOT analysis

Competitor Analysis

If you live in an area that has a lot of food trucks, you're not going to have trouble finding competitors to analyze. The trick is to pick the right ones. Food trucks come and go, just like restaurants do. You need to pick the strongest of the bunch and reverse-engineer their business models until you know them almost as well as the owners do.

You'll need a spreadsheet to keep track of everything related to your competition. The most obvious data points are their menus and food styles. Note their prices and any loyalty programs they're offering. Go ahead and eat their food as well while you're at it. Keep a log of their locations over the past six months. If you live in an area that has cold weather, note how they managed that season. Perhaps they have a catering service that kept them afloat during that time? Or did they change their menu?

The easiest way to figure out their location is to take a look at the Instagram page. All food trucks have social media accounts with geolocation tags on. This helps bring prospective customers in. It also makes it easy for you to figure out where the top locations are. Mind you, you don't have to copy their location patterns. These places will be extremely competitive, so they might not be the best choice for a newbie food truck operation.

Note how long they've been in business. Their website will list this. The longer a truck has been around, the better their reputation is and the more word of mouth advertising they have. In some ways, it can be counterproductive to study trucks that have been operating for a long time. They've built enough equity with their customers that they can take a few risks with locations and menu choices that a new business can't.

This is why it's better to have a spectrum of competitors. Choose one that has been around for a long time, one that has been around for a year or so, and another that has been recently launched and has been generating a lot of buzz. You'll be able to find these new entrants through media mentions. Search Twitter for mentions of food truck names. The ones that show up the most are the most popular. Look at when their Instagram posts first began and you'll get a good idea of how long they've been around.

Here are the data points you need to collect, in addition to the ones already mentioned:

- Marketing channels
- Target customer - You'll have to guess, but visiting the truck a few times and examining their feeds will give you a decent idea. You don't need a persona, just a few demographics.
- Average price point
- Foot traffic at locations per hour
- Estimated revenues
- Advertising voice and style
- Strengths
- Weaknesses
- Your advantages over them - Food quality is one but you want to look for something more than this.

- Their advantages over you - This is crucial. It'll prevent you from running away with yourself.

The objective with this analysis isn't to see if they're better than you. Just conduct it with the intention to get to know their business fully. Think of yourself as a business analyst whose job it is to figure stuff like this out. Rinse and repeat for all of your chosen competitors. Run it for at least three businesses, as mentioned earlier.

Note that this business analysis doesn't stop once you've completed your marketing plan. There are always new competitors on the scene and you need to stay up to speed. A deep-pocketed new entrant has the potential to blow you out of the water if you're not careful. So always stay up to speed with your market, even though it can be tough to do this when you're running a business.

However, this is what is needed to make this business a success. Most unsuccessful owners aren't willing to carry out these tasks. Doing this is what separates you from their ranks.

SWOT Analysis

SWOT stands for Strengths, Weaknesses, Opportunities, and Threats. It's a highly useful analysis to conduct since it forces you to be as objective as possible about your business prospects. Start off by compiling a list of strengths associated with your business. Qualities such as your food, operations, ownership structure, and so on are valid business strengths. If your cuisine addresses a gap in the market, this is a strength as well.

If you're the only one serving a type of cuisine in the market, you need to take a long hard look at why this is. Don't naively assume that you're smarter than everyone else. For example, if you're a New Yorker and find that no one's serving Korean food at a particular location, it's probably because no one wants that style of food there. There are enough Korean food businesses in the city and the odds of you being the only one who's found this gap is close to zero.

Look for some of the tell-tale signs of a cuisine that's just not in demand. One of these signs is the presence of a decent sized community that consumes this food but there are a lack of restaurants. This means, the community isn't big enough to support a business that cooks this type of food, and people outside the community aren't interested in it. Ideally, you want to see a small number of food trucks operating in the cuisine, but not too many.

If you find a large number of trucks operating, this doesn't mean you should give it up. Instead, look at how you can niche yourself within it. I provided examples of doing this previously in the book. You could be the dessert food truck or breakfast food truck, and so on. As a rule of thumb, try to avoid being a pioneer at anything. Food tastes are fickle. You might see huge demand at first as people are curious about the cuisine. However, you won't know how many truly like it until the next few weeks. Instead, it's better to operate in a niche that has demand and less competition. If competition is too high, niche yourself to reduce competition.

This is why your strengths and weaknesses tie with one another. It's very easy to assume a quality of yours is a strength when it's actually a weakness. Poor execution can make a strength a weakness as well, so make it a point to note what makes a quality a strength or a weakness. Food freshness can be a huge strength. Delivering this requires great process execution. Without it, it's a weakness if you're claiming fresh food but are delivering re-heated slop.

Be honest about your weaknesses. By "your", I mean your business, not you. If you identify that marketing is a weakness, figure out how you can address this or mitigate it. Perhaps hiring someone to manage your social media is a good idea? It costs money but you'll earn it back through increased orders. To run a good business, you need to be able to delegate work properly. Many first-time business owners struggle with this. If delegation is your weakness as a manager, list it and work to mitigate it.

Next, it's time to list the opportunities your business has to stand out from the crowd. This is where your competitor analysis report will come in handy. Take a look at the gaps in their operations and execution. This spells opportunity for you. Could you design an app that can deliver updates faster to your customers than mere social media? Investing in an app is a notable expenditure, but it does a ton to build a wonderful experience for your customer. You can collect payment, collect orders online, deliver customer loyalty points, and also inform people of your location without having to rely on just social media.

Your app can also function as a feedback collection machine. You can run contests and have people vote on what they'd like to see added. Best of all, you can create a community using your app. This is what consumers want the most, so give it to them. If no one else is doing this, or if they're not doing it well, there's your opportunity.

The final portion of your analysis is threats. Threats are items or occurrences that can disrupt your business. For example, bad weather is a threat, as is a lack of social media presence. Inability to execute your processes are prominent threats and can turn strengths into weaknesses. When listing process-related threats, make sure you get as specific as possible. For example, not having your lunch meal prep done by 11AM is a threat. There are many processes that are a part of that, so break those threats down as well.

This gives you a clear roadmap of processes you need to execute in order to succeed. It makes it easy for you to refer back to them when you're confused or are unsure if your business is on the right path. As your business grows, the threats against it will evolve as well. So make sure you're updating your analysis as often as necessary. Don't make the mistake of creating a document once and then forgetting about it.

Creating an Overview

Once you've completed this foundational work, it's time for you to create an overview of your marketing plan. This is a high-level look at what your plan is all about. Don't get caught up with the details here. Here are the sections your overview plan needs to have:

- Mission statement - Why does your business exist and what is its USP? Why will a customer choose your food truck over someone else's?

- Elevator pitch - You might be pitching your business to investors one day, so it's a good idea to be prepared with an elevator pitch. This is a 60-second pitch of what your business is about, its value, and why it's a great deal. This should be less than 130 words ideally.
- Marketing tone - What will your voice be like in your marketing campaigns? If it makes sense to you, create a marketing persona for your business. You don't need to officially have a mascot but that's what you're creating. Think of your mascot as being the personification of your business. How will this character talk, behave, and convince people to come to your food truck? Maintain this tone throughout your campaigns so that customers have a consistent experience.
- Goals - Where do you want to be within a year? Have revenue goals, customer count goals, number of social media followers, and so on. Customer retention is also a good goal to track. How many of your customers are repeat buyers? Think of ways you can measure this. Don't write the method down here but brainstorm ideas to track this metric.

Feel free to add anything else you think is relevant to your business. It's your marketing plan after all!

Creating Your Marketing Plan

Your marketing plan is going to have different sections in it which I'll detail shortly. Before we get to the sections though, you need to create a template for organizing them in place. With this template, all you'll need to do is fill relevant information in that you can quickly refer to down the road. This is opposed to writing free-form text plans that are difficult to read in a hurry.

Here is the framework or template within which you'll organize information:

- Goal - Each section is a strategy and every strategy has to support one of your primary goals. You identified these goals in the overview previously. Write down which goal the marketing strategy targets.

- Audience - If you have three of four customer personas, write down which persona is being targeted here. If you have just one then you can write their name down here.

- Channels - Using information from the previous two points, which channel makes the most sense. If your aim is to drive foot traffic towards a location at a music festival, and if your relevant persona will be attending this festival, which platform will they be using? Instagram is the most popular, but in this case TikTok also makes sense. Would Twitter make sense? Brainstorm options in this manner.

- Timeline - When do you plan on hitting your goals? Are there any key milestones you wish to hit? When will you hit them?

- Metrics - What are the key indicators you'll use to measure progress towards your goal? Make sure they're easily measured and aren't designed to boost your ego. If you can find them, include the baseline measurements for each metric so that you can compare your progress against them. For example, if you're running paid ads, what is a good click-through rate (CTR?) The exact number varies, but there are industry-wide averages you can measure yourself against.

- Responsibilities - Who will execute the tasks related to this section? What is their role? Write their name down as well. If you have employees this makes it easy for them to understand what your expectations are.

- Budget - How much money will you spend on this particular item? How will you measure the return on money spent? With some marketing tactics, it's not easy to measure your ROI. Consider implementing a feedback system for your customers. When they order, have them specify how they heard about you. Another method is to provide different checkout or discount codes for different platforms and strategies. Customers will use these and you can track their usage easily. Divide the profits you generated from each channel by the money you spent on it and you'll have a clear ROI measurement.

I'd like to mention that you don't have to know all of these components in advance, or that you even need all of these components in your template. It's your business so prioritize what makes sense for you. If you find that a free-form text approach works better instead of an organized section like this, then go for it. As long as you have a way of tracking the return on your efforts, it's worthwhile. Here are the strategies you can use to promote your business. These will be individual sections in your marketing plan.

PR/Media Mentions

Journalists are always on the lookout for great stories. Think about what makes your food truck great and pitch this to journalists. There are different ways you can stand out in their eyes. The most reliable way is to present a human interest angle. Have you ever turned on the cable news and seen some feel-good story? Journalists eat these kinds of stories up. In your case, it could be a story connected to yourself or some item on your menu. Perhaps your grandmother inspired a dish that has been long-lost or perhaps it's a new take on it. Everyone has great stories to tell, so brainstorm what makes your story special.

The second method is to tap into what's trending. Environmental sustainability is important right now so pitch this to journalists. Perhaps your food containers are biodegradable or your food is sourced locally, and so on. Appealing to customers based on current trends is always a great marketing ploy.

Cooking techniques or certain food crazes are also great to take advantage of. Remember the excitement that gripped New York City when the cronut was released? Every bakery in the city took advantage of it, not least the original inventor of the treat. While that was an exaggerated event, there are local crazes that grip people in the same way. Take advantage of this.

Remember that your marketing plan isn't something you implement just upon launch. It's a continuing plan of action. Focus on your employees and on your customers. Perhaps there's one customer who keeps returning all the time. Get to know them well. Who knows if they might have a story that can boost your popularity? It could happen indirectly as well.

For example, there was recently a news story about an 89-year-old pizza delivery driver who received a donation of $12,000 from one of his regular customers. The customer loved ordering from the local Papa Johns where the driver worked. While the story mentioned the restaurant tangentially, you can bet that the establishment received increased traffic thanks to the story. Always be on the lookout for such opportunities.

Events

Special events are a potential gold mine for you. They attract a ton of people and all of them need food. If you've ever visited a music festival, you know the kinds of crowds you can expect. They're also a perfect opportunity for you to go viral. Create an event calendar ahead of time so that you'll know when to begin preparing for it. Every event has its own little marketing method so you'll need to figure out what you can do for each one.

Creating a one-off hashtag for an event and prompting your customers to use it is a great way to increase follower counts and engagement. Another strategy to use is to partner up with other food vendors at the event. If someone sells an item that complements yours, you can partner up and offer a discount on the combined order. You'll need to work out how the margins will work with the other owner, but these partnerships are extremely common. In fact, you'll find other owners reaching out to you when you sign up for your first event.

You could even consider creating special packaging for the event and prompting customers to use it in unique ways to highlight your business. Provide giveaways or incentives for people to share and interact with you on social media. For example, a hashtag mention gets them a free soda. Some food trucks place screens on their exteriors that display the latest tweets and Instagram mentions. The chance to see themselves on the screen is a great incentive for people to interact with you on social media.

You can create giveaways and incentivize people to sign up via special landing pages. This is particularly relevant if you have another business linked to your food truck. Many food truck vendors run catering businesses as well. If someone has a wedding or a function coming up, you can prompt them to sign up at your link. Another option is to offer customers a chance to win a week's worth of meals at a discount.

This might be tough to pull off without the right delivery infrastructure, but you could offer them seven meals, one per day for the next week, and ask them to sign up and pay through a landing page or on your website. Not only will you capture their emails for further communication, you'll also receive pre-orders for the next week. Combine this with the usual earnings you'll make and it's a big boost to your business.

As your business matures, you can use your food truck at events such as these to build second businesses that can sustain themselves like this. This builds two streams of income for you, which is something that most food truck owners would die for.

Branding

Branding is something you need to do by default, but the methods of doing it can be different. They offer you a chance to stand out from the crowd. Most food trucks opt for vinyl wrapping. This is not a DIY method so you'll need to hire outside help and this costs money. The positive aspect is that you can create consistency across all of your marketing channels. If you happen to have a complex logo and art, vinyl wrapping your truck might be the best way to go.

The other option is to hand paint it. This is a time-consuming task and most food truck owners aren't expert painters. This means you'll be unlikely to paint anything beyond a few basic shapes. The positive aspect is that it's cheap. It also offers you a way to stand out from the crowd. You can hire a local artist or artists to paint your truck and use this publicity to drive traffic. If your food is already sourced locally and has a sustainable theme to it, this is a great tactic to drive customers to you.

You could opt for both methods for practical purposes. This particular method won't work for everyone but consider having aspiring artists paint your truck every week or every month. It gives them free publicity and it keeps your truck looking fresh. There are logistical challenges to this but it's worth a shot.

Apps

I've mentioned the benefits of apps previously. They give you an opportunity to truly own your customer so you should consider launching one of your own. You don't need to hire developers to create one for you from scratch. You can opt for what's called a white-label solution. You'll be given a template app that does everything you want. All you need to specify is the branding you need and other elements you'd like changed. The final app is delivered to you and it looks and feels like something you created. TouchBistro is an example of a white-label app provider.

The best part of an app is the analytics kit that you'll receive. These platforms allow you to track your customers' behavior on your app, and you can make better decisions regarding marketing and other features of your business.

Website

Every business needs to have a website these days. You might think that between an app and a social media account, you don't really need a website. This is the wrong attitude to take. A web presence is a lot like buying a piece of property these days. You stake your presence on the web and can claim it as being truly yours.

Your website will also come equipped with a blog and you can use this to drive traffic to your business organically. This is done through search engine optimization or SEO. SEO takes a while to truly get going, but once it does, it's a great way to generate free traffic. You can even turn your website into a store and sell some of your sauces and other menu items through it. For example, your customers might be enquiring about a specific sauce you use in your food. Bottle it up and sell it through your website! You can't do that through a social media account.

You can list your menu on your website and also list recipes, locations, conduct polls and publish your event calendar. Maintaining an active blog is a good way to keep Google happy and it will send people your way. There are many monetization opportunities with a website. For starters, you can run ads on the site if your page views are high enough. Next, you can consider publishing a cookbook with your recipes in it. Other products such as t-shirts, hats, and hoodies are popular as well.

It all begins with starting a website. Get one set up and the monetization opportunities will take care of themselves. As your business matures, keep returning to this section of your plan and keep updating it.

Social Media

This is a big one. It's also the biggest opportunity you have to get ahead of your competitors. The reason is that most food truck owners are extremely busy with their food and menu and don't take social media as seriously as they ought to. They dabble in it or engage it without specifying any goals. This is a mistake. Fix your goal before you begin using social media.

Next, hire someone to manage your social media for you. Don't hand your accounts over to your niece just because she knows her way around Twitter and Snapchat. You need someone who has marketing chops. They need to understand what your tone is and who your customers are. Without this, your marketing effort is wasted. Once you have the right person, confirm their duties and how you'll monitor them. You should have clear metrics installed right in the beginning that are in line with your goals.

Once all this is done, you can begin exploring which platforms make the most sense to you. Instagram is an obvious choice but there are other channels you should be present on as well:

- Twitter - This is the second most popular platform for food trucks. It allows you to post instant location updates and get in front of your customers easily. It provides your customers with another point of contact, so it's a great channel to utilize. Do not get political or religious. Leave that to the news media.
- Foursquare - Not many people use this but its audience skews younger. It's a great way to share your location with users. You don't have to use it but there's no harm in seeing if it works for you.
- Pinterest - Pinterest is a visual search engine and women are its primary users. It works for pretty much every niche, so it's a great way for you to expand your business' reach. You can create great infographics along with your photos and link your Twitter, Instagram, and Pinterest accounts to one another. This gives customers three points of touch before they visit you.

- YouTube - A hugely underrated platform for food truck owners. YouTube is the second largest search engine in the world and you should be posting content on it. Its video format makes your business real to your customers and you can help them feel the vibe at your location. You don't need any fancy video production teams. Make it real and create engaging content. Let users take a peek behind the scenes as you make their food, let them know how your day is spent, and so on. This humanizes your business and brings people closer to you. This is the fourth point of touch for your customer.
- LinkedIn- This platform is ideal for business conversations. You can network with commercial kitchen owners and investors on the platform. Ditch the marketing tone of your brand for a formal/businesslike tone that is appropriate to the platform.

You'll notice I haven't mentioned Facebook. This is because Facebook doesn't make sense for new businesses anymore. The platform runs on paid ads and it doesn't matter how much content you post, or how great it is, your organic reach is extremely low. You can establish a Facebook page down the road but in terms of ROI you'll see better results from the platforms I've just mentioned.

TikTok and Snapchat are still platforms that no one has quite figured out as yet. TikTok is going viral and is full of teens dancing to music they didn't create. It's hard to see a food truck connection here but if your food appeals to kids, it might be a good way to promote your business. Snapchat has a slightly older audience, but they're young compared to the rest of the platforms. You don't have to be present on it but, exploring it might give you a good idea of whether it works or not.

Social media can give you at least four points of touch with your customer. In marketing, a customer is thought to need eight points of touch before they decide to buy your product. When you combine social media with your other marketing efforts, you'll see foot traffic increase massively. The great thing about social media is that you can refresh your content regularly and this keeps engaging your customers. Cross-sharing your content also keeps you fresh in your customers' minds.

Consider going live on YouTube or Instagram. This type of content is promoted heavily by both platforms and you'll be able to share live feeds of your truck with your customers. Use stories and filters to keep your content fresh. Hopefully, you can now see why you need someone to manage your social media full-time. Use it well and you'll have a leg up on your competitors, who are busy worrying about costs.

Email Newsletters

Email seems like a blast from the past but it's still extremely relevant for businesses. Email marketing is one of the most effective methods of advertisement. Research indicates that close to 36% of email subscribers read newsletters to stay up to date with a publisher's content (Crook, 2019) You can use email marketing to stay in touch with your customer and to promote your social media and web content.

This form of marketing is especially useful if you're planning on running a promotion or a giveaway. The best part of email marketing is that you don't need to create special content for it. Put together the best performing content over a week into a newsletter, let the reader know what your plans are for the upcoming week, and you'll have a fully fleshed out newsletter ready to go.

Contests

People love winning stuff so why not allow them to do so? Set a clear goal for your contest before running it. Your aim should be to increase sales or increase brand awareness. The latter result is hard to measure so it's better to stick to something tangible like sales. Set expectations clearly with your customers and promote your contest through your channels.

You could offer a free meal to someone who wins your contest. For example, anyone who posts the best content tagging you on social media could win a free ice cream or drink. You can pick a user at random to offer a free meal to. You could also run a promotion where the 99th person to visit your truck gets a free meal. This is certain to drive traffic to your truck. You'll need to track customer orders. It doesn't have to be just the 99th, you can choose random numbers to keep people guessing.

If you happen to serve extremely spicy or extremely large portions of a certain item, you can hold eating contests. Chicken wing restaurants do this all the time so you can replicate that concept. There's no dearth of competition ideas, so do your research. You can even collaborate with other food trucks to offer a joint promotion.

Online Reviews

Nothing drives traffic quite like online reviews. First, make sure your website is indexed by Google and can be found. Google does this automatically so you don't need to do anything special. Once done, prompt your customers to leave you reviews. Let them know on social media and plaster the message on the side of your truck. Let them know how important it is for your business' growth. Your customers will oblige.

If you don't prompt them, they're unlikely to leave reviews. Yelp used to be extremely popular and still is. However, more people are turning to Google reviews these days so make use of that. You can monitor online reviews to get an insight into what your customers are thinking. Respond to their reviews as much as possible, especially negative ones, so that you come across as a business that cares.

Tips to Keep in Mind

Here are a few tips that will help you craft a winning marketing plan:

- Create a community - The best businesses have a community feel to it. Your customers want to feel as if they're a part of something bigger. In an increasingly online world, finding human connection is tough. Give this to them by presenting a human touch to your business.
- Take great photos - Since your primary social media channels are visually driven, you need to take great photos of your business. Whether it's of your truck, your food, or your location, taking eye-catching photos is a great way to boost engagement.
- Promote your schedule - Publish your event calendar and location listings. Make it as easy as possible for people to find you.
- Pin yourself- Create a Google Maps pin for yourself so that people can always find you. Update this as your location changes. You don't want people searching for you and driving to the wrong address.

Boosting Marketing Efforts

Once your marketing plan is in place and you've been executing it successfully, use these boosts to get even better results. Ideally, you'll have them in place from the start but this isn't always necessary.

Make it Fun

Create an atmosphere of fun when your customers interact with you. A good way to do this is to incorporate secret menus or to provide them with random freebies. Secret menus give customers a feeling of belonging to a special community and it separates them from regular customers. They also make your task of identifying a long-time customer easier. Provide these customers with additional incentives to keep coming back and your business will grow.

Be Healthy

People are increasingly health conscious these days so providing healthy options is a no-brainer. In many cases, announcing that your menu has become healthier will drive more traffic to you. People want to see calorie counts and other nutritional data with their food, so give it to them.

Customize

Customization is a tricky thing to get right. You want your customers to have a choice but you don't want them to effectively cook their own food. A customer isn't an expert in what tastes good. They might end up mixing sauces together and creating something disgusting. Needless to say, they won't be back. Use customization selectively by guiding customers through choices where they won't create something terrible.

Go Behind the Scenes

Engage

Engage with your customers and accommodate their needs as much as possible. Customers these days are increasingly turning vegan so providing such options in your menu is critical. Create polls and seek feedback from them. Keep the conversation going with them. They'll feel as if they're with you on your journey and will reward you with their business.

Go Mobile

You're on a truck so you're already mobile. However, are you digitally mobile? Offering mobile ordering solutions and payment methods is critical to your success. Mobile usage is increasing every day and people are using digital wallets, apps, and other data on their phone to make choices. Offering them a seamless ordering and customization solution will set you apart from your competition.

Be Seasonal

Incorporating seasonal elements to your menu keeps it fresh and keeps customers on their toes. If you happen to have a menu item that is extremely popular, think twice before removing it. It could lead to a backlash against you. However, changing your menu with the season makes you more sustainable and it gives people another reason to visit your business and sample your food.

Partner

A great way to push the local and sustainable theme of your business is to partner with local businesses. I've already highlighted how partnering with artists can boost your presence. Show your support for a local business or even allow them to advertise their services on your truck. Showcase the local farm or store you're buying supplies from and ask them to return the favor (once you have credibility.) All of this makes you more relevant to the customer and you might even score discounts from your suppliers.

Create Event Calendars

Special events will boost your revenues massively. They cost money but the expense is worth it. Create and publish your calendar. Share it with your followers and let everyone know where you're going to be.

Deliver

Installing a delivery process is painful and the early days will be a headache. You want to partner with services such as Deliveroo, Uber Eats, or GrubHub at first. They'll take a cut of your sales but you'll be able to access more customers. It goes back to offering more convenience to your customers. Give them many options, and they'll keep coming back to you.

Text

Texting is not something many people engage in these days but when it comes to marketing, many customers respond to business texts. Using a software such as Zipwhip, you can create automatic text sequences. Another option is to create a Facebook page and install a chatbot. There are many plugins that allow you to build your own chatbot.

For example, if a new customer visits your Facebook page they'll want to see your menu, your location, and your ratings. By building these options into a menu within the bot, this person can quickly decide whether they want to order from you or not. You can even have the bot send you orders and collect payments.

These kinds of experiences are what you should aim for. Customers love the convenience and you'll make more money. Best of all, these types of software don't cost much at all.

Press Releases

Press releases are a great way to get your business' information in front of editors and newspaper journalists. Services such as PRweb and PR Newswire allow you to craft your own press releases and send it to various outlets. There is a specific format to press releases that media outlets prefer. This format is quite simple. You can either write them yourself or have a professional writer craft one.

The press release begins with a title followed by a date and place. The first paragraph is the introduction. This is where you'll answer the who, when, where, and why questions surrounding the topic. Its aim is to indicate why this piece of news is important. The main body comes after this. Here's where you'll quote any statistics as necessary, information about your business, and further relevant material.

After the body comes the boilerplate section. This is where you'll talk about your own business along with your relevant social media profiles. Keep this to three to four lines. Include your contact information and all social media handles as necessary. Insert "####" at the end and center it to indicate the release has ended.

Your press release is not a story. It's a factual rendering of a piece of news. Journalists will use them in their own stories. Make sure you follow the format specified above. Editors are sticklers for formatting and any deviation will lead to instant rejection. Craft your press releases around relevant talking points and you'll find yourself being quoted in popular news stories. This will serve as free publicity for you and your business.

Chapter 7:

Location - Where to Park and

Where to Meet Your Customers

You can carry out all the marketing you want, but if your food truck isn't present at the right location, you're not going to do much business. You need to make it as easy as possible for people to find you and this is where location plays an important role. The right location can overcome less than optimal marketing. However, a poor location cannot be improved by great marketing.

Before diving into the specifics of location choice, you need to ask yourself some basic questions about your prospective locations. The first question to ask is whether you need additional permits or fees to do business in that location. Some high traffic locations, such as downtown areas, require additional permits and these can erase your margins. It's best to take some time to observe potential traffic at these locations. This is as easy as sitting in front of a food truck with a clicker and measuring the number of people served.

Check with your local food truck association or other food truck owners operating in the area about licensing requirements. Bathroom presence is a big deal in the food truck world and many optimal locations get disqualified because of this. You might find yourself stuck near a dingy alley where no one is going to find you. This brings me to the next point, which is space. High traffic areas are crowded and you'll need to make sure your truck fits the space you want to use.

Take note of the trucks already operating in the area. If you see vehicles that are similarly sized as yours, you're good to go. If you don't see many this could be a function of the space allocated to food trucks.

You might find that larger trucks are placed in a less than optimal location.

Foot traffic is crucial when it comes to evaluating locations. Keep in mind that there are low foot traffic pockets within high traffic destinations. For example, if you're in a park near a tree that provides a ton of shade, you're going to attract more people than a truck that is in the middle without shade nearby. This doesn't mean you can't do business from the second location but it's just that such locations aren't optimal. Even worse, you'll be charged the same amount no matter where you park.

The final point to consider is your competition. Do you want to be near them or away from them? A cluster of food trucks is always better but there are advantages to having a monopoly over a single location. When you're starting out, it's best to choose a cluster since it'll help spread the word easily. Also, a cluster of trucks validates your choice of location. One truck owner can be wrong but five of them being wrong about a location simultaneously isn't likely.

It's best to hoof it to the location and observe it yourself. Carry a clicker with you to measure the flow of customers at a truck of your choice. If the truck you're measuring serves your cuisine, think of how this will impact customer flow. If you're going to compete against them directly, you'll be reducing the flow in half for both of you. If you complement their cuisine, you can expect the same numbers as them.

If the location is good enough, ask yourself whether tweaking your menu choices makes sense. If not, you'll be better off serving at another location. Observe how popular each truck is at the location. If one truck is monopolizing all the traffic this is a telling sign that you'll face stiff competition there. Why would you want to go up against well entrenched competition right off the bat? Your odds of success aren't high in this situation. Instead, see if you can complement their menu in any way and drive some of their traffic towards you.

Locations That Always Work

There are some evergreen locations that always work for food trucks. If you can land yourself one of these spots, you'll do a decent level of business. Keep in mind that the authorities are aware of the attractiveness of these locations so you'll have to fork over hefty fees. However, the foot traffic more than makes up for it.

Food Truck Parks

These are no-brainers, even if you're a well established truck. When you're starting out, the presence of a few well established trucks next to yours is a great boost for your business. People will associate their quality with yours and the increased foot traffic will allow you to expand your marketing reach.

Keep in mind that you'll need to deliver great food. No one wants to be the person that lets the side down. If you're surrounded by great trucks you'll need to work hard to make sure your food is up to the challenge. The owners of these parks usually keep an eye on the spread of cuisines available. If you're serving Indian food and there's a truck that's already doing that, you're unlikely to get a spot.

Applying to a food truck park is a nice way to gather feedback about the popularity of your cuisine. You don't want to rely on just this method of measuring popularity, but if you find that the authorities are less than enthusiastic about your food, it means you're not going to have much demand.

Farmers Markets

The people who shop at farmers markets are interested in fresh, local produce. By setting up shop in one, you'll communicate your commitment to locally sourced products and sustainable food practices. You'll also be able to score some good deals from the suppliers present there. Journalists usually trawl farmers markets to mine stories and your presence makes it likely they'll get in touch with you.

Business Districts

Lunchtime is a highly lucrative business opportunity for food trucks in business areas. Office workers don't have too much time off, usually an hour to eat their food. If you can serve delicious food quickly, then you'll have a steady stream of customers. Enable online ordering and food pickup, and you have a winning formula.

Gas Stations

These aren't the most hygienic of places but you'll always find people looking for food at them. Instead of settling for the cold snacks in the convenience store, your hot food will entice people to your truck. If you're serving everyday food that is recognizable, such as burgers, hot dogs, or sandwiches, you'll do great business.

Bars

What happens after someone spends a night out with friends drinking? They rock up to a food joint to eat greasy food and have silly arguments. You don't need to seat these people, so their arguments won't cause you any damage. Sell them your delicious food instead and you'll gain a reputation as being the best late night spot to head to.

Festivals

I've already highlighted how great festivals and special events are. Park your truck at these events and you're guaranteed to sell a lot of food.

College Campuses

While college kids don't have a lot of money, they do need to eat a ton of food. They're also less picky about having a chair and table to eat, so food trucks are great choices for them. Make sure your menu is affordable. Don't compromise your margins by using cheaper produce or cuts of meat to reduce your costs, serve delicious food and you will be rewarded with regular customers.

How to Pick a Location

You're best served picking locations around the time you start dreaming up your business' name and cuisine. It's best to pick a few locations beforehand since this will give you a good idea of what cuisine will work and how big your truck needs to be (or how small.) You'll waste less time this way. Often, you'll find food trucks choosing their locations after they've done everything else only to find that their truck violates local laws.

You risk hurting your reputation, not to mention your wallet, by doing this. Conduct location research as you research local laws and ordinances. This will make your life a lot easier. Make it your objective to spot at least four locations that suit you.

Evaluating a Location

As I mentioned earlier, it's best to evaluate a location on foot. If possible, replicate a potential customer's journey to your location. In most American cities, you can do this by travelling by car, and then walking to the location. In some cities such as New York or Boston you'll have to use public transport and then find the location. Replicating this journey makes it easy for you to slip into your customer's shoes.

There are a few characteristics you need to look for when researching a space. The first is the size of it. If there are no food trucks around, can you park one in it? If there are other trucks around, what are their sizes? If you see no trucks around, this is probably because the local government doesn't allow them to operate from that location. Don't waste your time scoping out potential locations. As I mentioned earlier, head straight to where food trucks are already operating.

The only exception to this rule is if food trucks aren't popular in your city or area. In this case, check with the government to see if your list of potential locations are admissible. When looking at a space, visualize what your food truck will look like in it. How will the customers queue up and how will you serve them? Will the line for the bathroom run into the line for your truck? This will disrupt your business.

Take note of the spacing between other trucks. If they're too close to one another, the slightest delay will cause people to switch lines. Do you want them to linger nearby and eat their food or do you want them to move on? How will you design this?

Visibility is another major quality you need to evaluate. If customers can't see your truck, they're not going to come to it. Consider your proposed color scheme when looking at a location. If you're going to be parked under a tree, and if your truck is painted dark green or has similar hues, you're not going to be very visible. If you're serving food at night, check the light sources nearby. If your location is too dark or looks unsafe, people won't come to it.

The next quality to evaluate is competition. While food trucks are a source of competition for you, you need to take into account the restaurants in the area as well. What kind of food do they serve? If there are no food trucks serving your type of cuisine, check to see if many restaurants do. Take any company cafeterias into account as well. People usually avoid them, but their mere presence indicates competition that you'll need to account for.

How convenient is your location to access? Evaluate this from your customer's perspective and you and your truck as well. Your customer will be on foot so it will most likely be easily accessible. However, consider what you'll need to do to pull up in that spot. Take waste disposal and water needs into account. The local government is not going to be very happy if you make a mess of the place.

Take note of any commercial space nearby that attracts a lot of people. For example, malls, shopping centers, nightlife venues, parks, and sporting arenas are great feeders of traffic. You don't need to be right up against these venues. Being within walking distance of them is also great. Make sure you observe the ebb and flow of traffic at these locations. While sporting events will draw a large number of people, you don't want to be dependent on such events. If the location has steady traffic even when the venue is empty, this is an indicator of a great location.

Scope out at least four potential locations in this manner. Once you've found a few good ones, make a rotation plan. Successful food trucks rotate between locations. After all, you're not a restaurant. Rotating locations also helps develop desire in your customers to eat at your truck again. If you were always there, they might take you for granted. Pick a maximum of two locations every day and develop a rotation schedule that works for you. Keep your meal preparation needs in mind when designing your location plan.

Over and above your regular locations, make it a point to attend special events. A lot of these events can be covered in an hour or two and will provide you with a nice boost in income. There are many events that food truck owners don't even consider. For example, attending the end of a local school's soccer game is an event where you'll earn a few additional sales for sure. This isn't a particularly onerous event and you can serve it in under two hours without disrupting your day. You'll need to modify your preparation process a bit but this isn't too troublesome.

Here's a non-exhaustive list of events that won't strike you as being "special" in any way, but will bring you good business nonetheless:

- Industrial shows and conferences
- Home shows
- Auctions
- Antique shows
- Craft shows
- Open houses
- Company picnics
- Church functions
- School functions
- Social club functions
- Children's sporting events

Popular Events

Aside from the list above, there are the usual suspects. The bigger the event is, the more competitive getting a spot is going to be. For example, getting a spot in an outdoor New Year's Day event is going to be tough. Many restaurants launch food trucks during this time so you'll have additional competition to deal with.

Music festivals are a slam dunk for food trucks. They last over multiple days and with people shuttling between concerts, food trucks are a perfect fit for them. Festival organizers usually prefer a mix of cuisines when considering applications. If you're proficient in a cuisine that is underrepresented in your local area, you'll gain admission easily.

Parades are another great source of customers for food trucks. Every community has a parade, so placing your truck along parade stops is a good idea. You can even theme your menu to special occasions to appeal to customers. For example, many food trucks release shamrock influenced menu items during St. Patrick's Day parades. Ethnic parades and festivals are also a natural fit. Organizers usually seek representation of all parts of a culture's cuisine. Art festivals might not be as raucous as music or other festivals, but they draw hungry crowds as well. Outdoor movie nights are also a great source of traffic.

Summer festivals involving wine, beer, music, or other attractions are great locations for food trucks as well. Check with your local government for a calendar of special events that you can apply for. You can even cater private events. You can leave it up to the host as to whether you want to pull up in your truck or not.

Applying to Festivals

As great as the special event locations are, you can't simply rock up and park your truck. There is a formal application process that you'll need to go through. The organizers are very aware of how attractive their proposition is for you and will charge you for it. These days you can expect organizers to seek a cut of up to 40% of your sales, which is close to exorbitant. Food truck owners respond by increasing their prices to maintain their margins.

This brings us to a vital point. Not every event or festival is a good fit for you. If you're serving hamburgers, you're not going to fit into a festival that promotes vegan living. Brand fit goes beyond mere choice of food. Given the way the industry works today, you'll need to pay 40% of your sales to the organizer. Some even charge a flat fee plus a cut of your revenue. This means your prices need to be hiked for you to make any semblance of a profit.

How will customers react to this? Let's say you need to increase your prices by 40%. If your average price is $12 per order, you'll need to increase it to $17. This is an acceptable increase. However, what if you're selling pizzas for $20? Your new prices will be $28. This hike is less acceptable. Will your customers be unhappy? Complaining about greedy festival organizers isn't going to cut much ice with your customers.

Before rushing into a festival, take some time to review all of this. Work out what your menu will look like or if you need to rework your menu with special one-off items. You can reduce your food costs and live with minimal price increases. Take a look at how many food trucks will be present at the festival as well. There's no template I can give you that will specify what an ideal number is, you'll have to sift through prior attendance records.

If the trucks that appeared last year are applying again (you can check with the owners or through your association) this is a good sign. If every applicant is new, it deserves further investigation. Organizers usually lean towards the greedy side and have high costs of their own that they need to bear. They don't care about how individual trucks do as long as they get to collect 40% of the money spent on food. Steer clear of greedy organizers.

The success of the festival impacts your brand as well. If the festival turns out to be a fiasco, you don't want to be associated with it. Examine the pedigree of the organizers and check the results of the previous year. Check attendance records and other relevant data. Did the festival receive good PR and did many media outlets cover it? This is a good sign. If a few local dailies covered it and left it at that, the organizing team isn't up to scratch and you're best off avoiding them.

It sounds strange to say this but you want the organizers to be selective about the trucks they let in. It shows they care about the quality of their customers' experience and this will help you make a positive impression as well. A key indicator of their concern is to inquire about the restroom facilities. Check if there were any issues during previous years. Issues point to a greedy organizing team.

Application

Here's the harsh truth. You'll be competing with almost every other truck in your area. In larger cities, you'll be competing for 10-12 spots with over 200 trucks. You need to be able to stand out and your track record is the easiest way to do so. The longer you've been in operation and the better your reviews are, the more likely it is that you'll be chosen.

Before applying, make sure you run all the numbers and design your menu. Given that people will be moving from one place to another, make sure your menu has quick turnaround times. You'll need to coordinate food prep with your commercial kitchen so all of your employees will need to be on point. Make sure you run the truck yourself when the day comes.

Your application should explain what your brand is, how long you've been in business, and your style of food. Include attractive photos of it and also highlight your reviews on Google and Yelp. Leave links to your social media and mention your engagement numbers if they're high. List your menu and mention how it's designed for a quick turnaround. It's better to assemble food than it is to cook it at a festival.

When the day comes, make sure your truck sparkles. Customers won't be eating inside your truck but looking at a truck that has mud stuck on its wheels or has mud splashed across its face will turn anyone's appetite off. Clean it thoroughly and do whatever it takes to keep it sparkling. Make sure you've applied and received the right permits. The organizers will help you receive the temporary food facility permit.

Focus on providing your customers with the best service possible, and they'll reward you with good reviews. Remember that your social media page should be active. Incentivize people to tag you and share relevant content about you. It'll be a whirlwind of activity for you to take in, but when done right, festivals will bring you massive social credibility.

You'll find that your foot traffic on regular days will increase because more people will be aware of your brand. Keep your food simple and ensure it's served quickly. The last thing you want is long lines forming because people are waiting to get served. Organizers will notice this and word will spread around. The most important thing for you to organize is your food supply chain. If you're at an all-day event, there's only so much food you can carry onboard your truck.

You can't close your truck and drive back and forth either. Customers will keep coming by throughout the day, so you will need to have food delivered to you constantly. Communication is key, so make sure your employees are up to speed on everything that needs to be done on the day. It'll be hectic as I said, but it'll be rewarding as well.

Chapter 8:

The Beating Heart of Your

Business - Your Menu

There are many important components of your food truck business, but none more important than your menu. Customers are ultimately going to judge you on how tasty your menu is. Your menu determines how successful you'll be, and also what level of service you can provide for your customers. A well-designed menu will leave customers hungry for more and reduces the burden on your shoulders.

A poorly designed menu will torpedo your business before it even gets off the ground. First time food truck owners are likely to get ahead of themselves when designing their menus. In the rush of starting a new venture, they're likely to go out and buy the most expensive ingredients, which will increase their costs. As a result, they'll price themselves out of the market. You can't compete against fine-dining restaurants from a food truck. So don't think you need to have the finest ingredients.

This doesn't mean your ingredients need to be bad. You need to draw the line somewhere and balance your desires with practicality. Cheaper cuts of meat and cheaper vegetables can be just as delicious as the more expensive ones. You need to get creative with how you cook them. Keeping the purpose of a food truck in mind, make sure your menu has a quick turnaround time.

General Tips

Quick turnaround times are crucial for food trucks since customers won't hang around forever. They're likely to queue outside a restaurant that serves great food, but this isn't the case with a food truck. There are so many other options consumers have that it doesn't make sense for them to do so. If you're targeting the lunchtime office crowd, no one is going to stand around for more than 10 minutes to get their food.

Brainstorm dishes that can be prepared in advance and need to be put together, or food that cooks quickly. If your dishes contain rice in them, this is something you can prepare well in advance. Sticking with the Mexican food example, as I have throughout this book, you would only need to assemble a burrito or a taco with cooked ingredients to produce a delicious dish. Other cuisines lend themselves to such organization as well. For example, if you're serving Indian food, you can precook all curries and rice beforehand and simply serve them hot when ordered. If you're serving burgers, you can cook them beforehand and keep them warm until customers order them. This is what fast food restaurants do. You'll be using better quality meat so don't worry about coming across as a fast food joint.

Another excellent way to reduce your expenses is to create a menu that uses a common set of ingredients. Not every dish on your menu needs to have the exact same ingredients but limit them to a small number. This makes shopping for ingredients a lot easier. By buying larger quantities of ingredients, you can buy them in bulk and this decreases your costs. It also reduces the chances of food going to waste, since your ingredients will be used in every dish.

The number of items on your menu is also a key factor. Most food trucks have between six and 12 items (*Hints for Building Your Food Truck Menu*, 2020). Remember that quality is better than quantity. Your customers aren't expecting a restaurant, so don't think you need to give them all kinds of food. Stick to the ones you can cook well and that they'll love. Besides, remember my earlier point about changing menus with the seasons. This gives you a chance to refresh your menu so you won't be stuck cooking the same things all year.

Your prices are affected by your costs. If you follow the previous tips, you'll automatically be able to set good prices that deliver value to your customers. Remember that you're running a business, customers will always go to whichever place gives them the highest value. Your food might taste great but there's a maximum price someone will be willing to pay for it. So don't let your ego set prices. Follow the tips in this chapter to set realistic prices and always keep your costs as low as you possibly can.

Menu Themes and Space Considerations

When picking the cuisine for your food truck, it can be hard to decide which one to pick. I've already mentioned how you need to go about narrowing down your options. If there are a large number of trucks serving your style of food, you can either niche down or change the type of cuisine you want to serve. Decide on the theme of your menu and start narrowing it down from there.

Every food truck has certain items that are pillars. They're the items that will be ordered the most and will convey everything that your truck has to offer. They need to be closely tied to the theme of your cuisine. They also need to be easy to cook and shouldn't require your customers to wait in long lines. This is quite a tall order. You could cook the item beforehand and store it in warm containers prior to serving but make sure the texture and flavor of the food is preserved.

Be realistic about how many items can be on your menu. You'll be working with a small staff (usually just two people, including yourself), and you'll be working in a smaller space. No matter how large your commercial kitchen space is, you're going to be serving food out of your truck. You'll still need to deliver great taste to your customers. It's a tough ask, so make sure you take the time to really think deeply about your menu.

The smaller your menu is, the higher its quality will be. However, you don't want to go too small since this will turn customers away. If this is your first time running a business, keep it below 10 items for your own sake. Once you've landed on a few items, it's time to test it out. Have your staff and family taste your dishes and time how long it takes you to serve them. Try to cook the dishes 30 seconds faster and see if this is possible.

In a real world environment, you'll likely have less time and more stress. This is why the 30-second test is a good one to implement. It trains you to move faster so when the real thing comes, you'll be up for it. Gather feedback from everyone who tastes your menu and incorporate it. If your food isn't up to it, take it on the chin and redesign your menu. Don't stick to your old menu stubbornly.

Incorporating feedback into your decisions is the key to succeeding in this business. You need to be innovative and turn a profit. You'll likely have to go through a few iterations of your menu before you land on the perfect combination. Streamline your options as much as possible. If you're serving grains, limit them to two options. If you're serving wraps, limit the number of items your customers can add.

You need to strike a balance between streamlining and offering no options at all, so be careful of this. Seek feedback from the people around you and incorporate it into your future designs. Once you've landed on a winning combination, it's time to price your food.

Setting Prices

Prices are a crucial component to your business. They determine your profit percentage and convey the degree of value you're giving your customers. You want your prices to generate a good amount of profit for yourself and leave you enough of a buffer to at least break even if things go wrong. As I mentioned earlier in this book, the usual approach is to multiply the unit cost of an item by three to arrive at the selling price.

Demand also plays a role. If your truck becomes well known for a certain dish, you can charge more for it. If you've noticed that a certain item is in high demand at a particular time of the day or due to the venue you're in, you can raise prices. Obviously, you don't want to extort your customers, be sensible with your price increases.

A food cost percentage model is also used by restaurants. Typically, the cost price of the food is anywhere between 20 and 40 percent of the sale price. If a menu item costs $2 to prepare, its sale price can be between $5 to $10. The 3X multiplication lands in the middle of this range. You want to increase or decrease your prices depending on how much time it takes you to prepare an item.

This method places a premium on your gross margins (remember them?) Your gross margin is calculated as follows:

Step 1: Sale price ($5) - Cost price ($1) = $4

Step 2: Divide result of Step 1 by Sale price → 4 / 5 = 0.8 = 80%

You want your gross margins to be as high as possible since this gives you more room to account for operating expenses. However, you can push prices only so high before customers rebel. You'll find that after accounting for sensible customer prices, your gross margins will land around 40-80%. If your gross margins are less than this, you need to have low operating expenses. An ice cream vending truck will have low operating expenses since there isn't much prep work that needs to be done other than making large batches and storing products. A truck that cooks fresh food will have higher operating expenses since inventory turnover will be faster.

You can target food costs to be a certain percentage of your menu price. Let's say you want food costs to be 30% of your menu price (which means your gross margin is 70%), and an item costs you $2 to make. Its sale price is calculated as:

Menu price = Cost price/Cost percentage = 2/0.3 = $6.66

Another way of approaching the question of menu pricing is to target a gross margin and see what prices you end up with. Let's say a menu item costs you $2 to prepare and you want to earn 50% gross margins on this item. The sale price can be calculated as:

Gross margin amount desired = Cost price/ Gross margin percent = 2/0.5 = $4

Menu price = Cost price + Gross margin price = 4+2 = $6

You'll need to check whether this item can reasonably sell for $6 per portion. If it's a plate of fries, no one's going to pay this much for them. If it's a burger, it's a steal. Food cost percentages and gross margins are two sides of the same coin. They add together to give you your final menu price. Play around with them to land at a price that makes sense for your customers and allows you to earn a good profit.

Closely related to this method is the factor pricing method. Here, you divide 100 by your food cost percentage and multiply this number by how much the food cost you. For example, if your desired food cost percentage is 30%, dividing this by 100 gives us 3.33 (100/30.) Multiply this by the cost of the item, let's assume this is $2, and you arrive at a menu price of $6.66.

Notice that the shortcut method that I mentioned earlier (multiply costs by three) assumes a food cost percentage of around 30% and a gross margin of 70%. To simplify calculations, simply multiply by three or 3.5 to arrive at a sensible menu price. If you can push it to a multiple of four, this is even better. Just don't sacrifice quality in the interests of profits.

A pitfall of using the shortcut is that it doesn't discriminate between low-cost and high-cost items. There are some items that will cost a lot and you won't have as high a gross margin on them. You can structure your menu in such a way that it has a mixture of high gross margin items and low ones. Given the way the industry works, you'll find that your primary menu items will be medium to low gross margin items. Accessory food such as sides, drinks, and simple desserts are high margin items.

To get an idea of how you can structure your menu, take a look at how fast food chains push products to their customers. They push combo meals because fries and Coke are high margin items. Restaurants can take a hit on the lower unit sale price of these items and still earn greater margins than the burger itself. Sides that can be turned into primary menu items are a gold mine. For example, loaded fries, loaded potatoes, and so on, have low costs and high gross margins. To load them you need to add just a few additional items and you have a massive earner. See if you can create little value additions to your sides to create main courses that can make you more money.

Menu Design

"Design" in this case refers to the physical design of your menu. You can have the most delicious food there but if customers don't like the way it looks, the taste of your food won't matter. Think of your menu as being an extension of the way your food looks. Would you eat anything on a plate that doesn't look fresh and delicious? Don't expect your customers to either. Here are some tips that will help you design a great menu board that will keep customers coming back for more.

Push Your Star Items

Our eyes are usually drawn to the upper right-hand corner of a board or to its center. Place your best dishes here. You can place your hero items in the center and highlight your highest margin products in the top right-hand corner.

Get the Visuals Right

We're visual creatures so it's important that the images associated with your food look great. Take pictures that make your food look as great as possible. Draw inspiration from how fast food chains photograph their food. Have you noticed a Big Mac on the menu board versus how it comes in a box? That's the standard you want to aim for. If you can afford one, hire a professional photographer.

If not, don't worry. Take photos with lots of light in them and edit the pictures using filters and other online software apps. These allow you to play around with the hues in your food to make it look more attractive. Don't go overboard with the edits since you want your photo to resemble the real thing.

Proofread

Always proofread your menu. The last thing you want to do is misspell the names of your food items. There's nothing more unappetizing than that. It also makes you look like an amateur. There are some clever food trucks that take advantage of misspellings to create humor and draw customers in.

These are fairly advanced marketing strategies. To break the rules, you need to learn what they are first. Avoid experimenting at first, and only start playing around with them once you're comfortable with how your customers think.

Descriptions. Not War and Peace

You love creating your food, so it's natural you'll want to describe it in great detail. Remember that your objective is to inform customers of what's in the dish. You're not writing a novel. If you're cooking ethnic food, remember the advice about restaurant names. You want some local flavor in the description, but put too much of it and no one will understand what they're ordering. Keep it simple and let your food do the talking.

Fonts and Colors

Be consistent with your fonts and colors. They need to tie-in with your branding. You will be tempted to run away with your fonts and use all kinds of them, but this will make you look unprofessional. Keep your font selection consistent across your website and your truck. Take a look at other websites and businesses that project the same marketing tone as you do. Look at their font selection and choose accordingly.

If you want to project a classy vibe, look at the website of Louis Vuitton and use their fonts. Don't use more than two fonts across your branding. You can search for fonts that complement one another and use those pairs.

Seek Feedback

Always have someone providing you with feedback. They can be your loved ones or your customers. If you have followers on social media, post your menu on your channels and ask them for feedback. Don't shy away from negative feedback. They're a means for you to get better.

Use Numbers

You can name your food items in as friendly a manner as possible, but if you're serving ethnic food, it's not always possible to make the item's name friendly to local speakers. Use numbers to identify meals and encourage your customers to use them. This will avoid them being embarrassed to order an item.

Label Dishes

If you're offering special dishes that are vegan, heart healthy, or anything else you can think of, make sure you label them. If you're serving ethnic food, indicate which menu items are spicy. Gluten-free, allergen information, and cooking methods are some of the other special methods that you'll need to clearly label.

Tricks That Enhance Your Menu

You can get as creative as you want with your menu. The challenge is to know when to stop. Overdo it and you'll draw attention away from the quality of your food. The idea with these tricks isn't to manipulate your customers. Instead, approach it with the intention of driving interest towards your food. You produce great food and your customers will enjoy eating it. So why not use certain psychological methods to help them make good choices?

Avoid Dollar Signs

You might be dreaming of dollar signs all day long but you don't want to show them to your customers. Menus that list dollar signs draw a customer's focus away from the food and onto the price. You want them to focus on the menu item and its description, not have them thinking about the price. List a number as the price and don't use any currency signs.

End Prices Differently

Visit a fast food chain and you'll notice that all prices end in "99." This is the hallmark of cheap stores. Everyone knows stores do this to make items look cheaper than they actually are. You want to use this principle but don't copy the "99" format. This will make you look cheap and customers will associate you with dollar discount menus.

Instead, end your prices with "95." It still makes your prices look cheaper than they really are and you'll avoid the bargain bin perception of your food.

Avoid Columns

What is the first thing you do when you see columns? Your eyes automatically start comparing features between all of them. This is why online services companies list their features in columns. It's easier to compare prices this way. That's not what you want with your menu. Listing your three best dishes as columns will lead to customers ordering the one that's priced the lowest.

Unless that's a deliberate ploy of yours, you want to avoid columns. Use lists instead and let your descriptions sell the item.

Bracket your Food

An exception to column usage is when you bracket your food. Bracketing is when you offer different sized portions of the same meal for different prices. It's a strategy that big food chains use all the time. You'll see the small size listed for $5, the medium for $7, and the large for $8. The portion sizes will be visually represented in columns and the large will look three times the size of the small but it's less than twice the cost.

Customers will naturally opt for the large since they'll consider the medium overpriced. You can use the same with just two sizes as well. Offer a small and large to your customers. The offer by itself will have them wondering whether the small will be enough to satisfy them. They'll order the large to avoid that risk. If the large is twice the size and priced at less than that multiple, they'll see this as grabbing a great deal and you'll see the larger portions more often.

Use the Top Right-Hand Corner

Not enough food truck owners do this and it's a shame. Always use the top right-hand corner of your menu board. Highlight your star items or your highest gross margin items on there. They'll sell a lot better and you'll make more money.

Use Great Photos

This is also something that most food truck owners neglect and it's baffling. People like to see pictures of the food they're about to eat before ordering for it. Take great pictures and highlight them in prominent areas around your truck. If you have printed menus, have enticing pictures on it to draw more orders.

Avoid Small Print

Have you ever read the description of a product and then noticed an asterisk next to it? Have you then scanned the rest of the page to try to figure out what the catch is? It's an annoying experience and it reminds people of legalese or complex financial documents. People are ordering food from you to relax and have a good time.

They don't want to be presented with complicated options that have caveats. Avoid small print literally as well. Don't make your menu too hard to scan or read from a distance. People will often scan a menu to figure out whether they want to eat there or not. Don't cram your menu with so much food that no one can figure out what's offered.

Be Consistent

If your menu carries one font and tone, your truck another, and your website a third, your customer is going to be confused as to what your offerings are. You need to be consistent across all of your channels. This is why it's helpful to hire someone to manage your social media and online channels. They'll ensure the tone is consistent and that the branding is on point.

Don't be a Bore

"Burger with cheese and lettuce." Or do you prefer, "Smoked burger topped with savory cheddar cheese and fresh lettuce?" The choice is obvious. Even if both of these descriptions refer to the same dish, you'll likely think that the second one is a world away from the first. It's challenging to create great descriptions and avoid writing overly lengthy descriptions. However, work in as many adjectives as you can.

Build a picture in your customer's mind. Visualize a picture that presents your food in the tastiest manner possible. Now write down some of the adjectives that come to your mind. Incorporate these into your description without going overboard. Avoid boring descriptions that make it seem as if you've thrown something together and are charging money for it.

Chapter 9:

Food Safety Essentials

Food safety will be your constant companion when your food truck is up and running. You're going to have to abide by all the relevant laws and the inspections that accompany them. If you're serious about your business, you'll prioritize food safety above all else. It's just good business. You don't want to be the food truck where people get poisoned.

Many restaurant owners adopt an antagonistic stance against food safety inspectors. This is completely pointless. The inspector isn't there to shut you down. They're simply there to ensure that hygiene is being maintained and that you're not compromising the safety of your employees and customers. They gain nothing by shutting you down so always strive to maintain the highest standards of food safety in your kitchen.

Check with the local health department to determine the frequency of food safety inspections. They usually occur once every year but you never know when a surprise inspection might occur. While local officials have health codes, the Food and Drug Administration (FDA) has its own set of guidelines. These are also enforced by local health department officials. The latest version of the FDA health codes can be found at https://www.fda.gov/media/87140/download.

Passing Inspections

Passing inspections is important but don't adopt the attitude that they're an exam you need to prepare for. Instead, understand that they're in place to protect you. If a customer of yours becomes ill, they may sue you in court. Do you really want to expose yourself to such processes? Think of what such a suit will do to your reputation. Ensure food safety is a part of your culture and you won't have any issues with the health inspector.

Train Staff

Make sure all of your staff is properly trained. This is necessary because everyone who works at a food handling facility needs to have proper instruction in best practices. Health inspectors will question staff during their inspections and if anyone shows ignorance of food safety practices, you could be hit with a violation. Make sure everyone on your staff understands the importance of food safety.

If you make it a point of work culture, your staff will follow suit. If you display laxity towards it, and treat it as a hurdle to jump or just an issue to outmaneuver, you're building a time bomb that is only going to lead you to trouble.

Wash

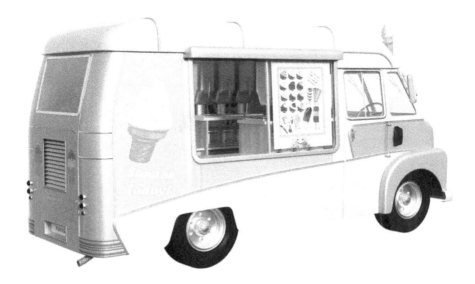

Food handling is a delicate operation. Touch a single spoiled food item and your entire kitchen can get infected. This is why it's critical for you to regularly wash your hands and change gloves. Be very careful to separate the food handling and money accepting functions in your business. Accepting money and handling food immediately after can expose your customers to food poisoning.

With the advent of digital payments, this problem is decreasing but you need to be very conscious of how you're handling these processes. Do not let the person handling food anywhere near the cash box when you're open. If you're the one handling cash and are passing food onto your customers, make sure the food is properly packed so that there's no contact with your hands.

Clean Produce

Produce, even locally sourced, travels a long way from farms to the kitchen. It's stored with food from other farms and is mixed with food of varying quality. They're transported in trucks of varying hygienic levels and by the time it reaches your kitchen, there's no telling where it's been.

It's prudent to wash all produce thoroughly. You can even purchase a special vegetable wash that removes all contaminants from the surface of the food. Ensuring that your produce is fresh is one thing. You need to make sure it's clean as well.

Proper Storage

It's easy to chuck things into the fridge and forget about them. Your storage practices need to be on point, and everything that you store in your freezer or fridge has to be labeled so that you know how fresh everything is. You're not going to sell out of food everyday so it's critical for you to make sure all of your food is appropriately stored and that you know how long their shelf life is.

Check the temperature of your fridge to make sure it's below 40F. Temperatures higher than this lead to bacterial growth that can cause food poisoning.

Sanitize

Everything that touches food must be sanitized before and after it touches food. Utensils, countertops, cutting boards, and even human hands need to be cleaned thoroughly before touching food. This is common sense but it can be easy to forget to do this in the rush of service. Establish clear policies that will ensure your employees will follow them at all times.

Inspect Supplies

Inspect your supplies thoroughly so that you're not buying less than ideal produce from your suppliers. As I mentioned earlier, food travels a great distance before it arrives at your kitchen so make sure it isn't contaminated before it gets there.

What Inspectors Look For

With the previous practices in place, you'll be in a great position to satisfy even the most fastidious of inspectors. There are a few key practices that every inspector evaluates in an inspection. Here they are in no particular order.

Handwashing

Contaminated hands are the biggest source of food poisoning in kitchens and it makes sense for inspectors to look for problems here. Make sure you and your employees always wash hands after touching unsanitized objects before touching food. A lot of this is common sense. Take care to cook vegan and meat dishes separately within your kitchen.

If you're advertising vegan options, you can't cook that food on the same surfaces or with the same utensils on which meat and animal products have been cooked. This isn't vegan food, after all. Your customers might not spot it but it's unlikely to pass the notice of a health inspector. Also, it's disrespectful to your customers to cook food in this manner. If it's a problem for you, don't serve vegan food. It's better than lying to them.

When you switch between handling produce and meat, make sure every surface is cleaned and sanitized. While cooking heat and deep cold kills most bacteria in meat, you can't be too careful. Review food safety instructions regularly so that your employees are up to speed.

Approved Sources of Food

A particular area of concern are your suppliers. While you need to follow correct food safety practices, your suppliers need to do so as well. Inspectors are extremely sensitive about the permits and licenses of your suppliers. If they're not a recognized vendor of food or aren't certified to be handling food, you can expect penalties to rain down on them and you.

Storage Temperatures

Inspectors will take a look at the temperatures of your food storage facilities. Make sure you inspect your fridges regularly to ensure there aren't any malfunctions. You'll be busy with the processes central to your business, so make sure you're not ignoring any issues with regards to food safety. Make sure all electronic storage facilities are routinely maintained and are cleaned.

Cross Contamination

Don't ever mix raw and cooked food together. This is a basic food hygiene practice but it's very easy to ignore it in the heat of the kitchen. You'll risk cross contamination by mixing them together so designate appropriate areas in your kitchen and within your truck where raw and cooked food needs to be handled.

These four items are the most critical things they'll look at. There are a number of other points that health inspectors will verify. While these aren't as critical, this doesn't mean they aren't as important.

Labeling

One of the keys to ensuring proper food safety is good labeling practices. All of your stored food needs to be labeled with the date it was cooked or bought. Write down the date and month on every container. Make sure you're sanitizing storage containers properly once they've been used.

Labeling also extends to your storage facilities themselves. Raw food should be stored away from cooked food. You can store them within the same fridge, but they need to be packed appropriately. Use your common sense here. Don't make the mistake of throwing everything together without labels or adequate packing into the same storage facility.

Permits

Yup, we're back to permits once more. They're a pain to research, applying for them takes time, and every government official is interested in them. While they're tangentially related to food safety, they are a part of doing business legally. Make sure all of your permits have been renewed and are up to date. You don't want to risk being shut down over an expired permit.

Instruments

Food trucks routinely use meat thermometers to make sure their food is properly cooked. A common cause of food poisoning is undercooking meat and poultry. Make sure your thermometers are working well and that you have backups. It's a good idea to use two thermometers to make sure everything is in working order. Food inspectors will verify temperature readings with instruments of their own, so be prepared for this.

Cleanliness

Cleanliness isn't so much an inspection item as much as it is a state of being. Everything in your truck and kitchen should be spotless. You need to clean everything after service, every time your kitchen is used. Many food business owners neglect cleaning since it's difficult to do. You've spent an entire day cooking food and the end of service brings a sigh of relief. You'll be tempted to relax and call it a day.

However, drill it into yourself and your staff that the day is not finished until every surface of your kitchen is cleaned and the trash has been disposed of. You don't need to clean the exterior of your truck every day, but as far as food handling surfaces, countertops, and utensils go, they have to be cleaned. Take care to clean the floors and the ceilings as well.

Grease often collects in these areas and as it builds up, dirt sticks to the surfaces. Cleaning these surfaces every night will ensure you avoid problems. If you're using ovens, friers, and other cooking pots, clean them every night with boiling water. Friers are especially critical since old grease collects in them. Many trucks use flat grills to cook food. Over time, a layer of carbonized food collects on top of them and will begin to coat all the food you cook. Scrape and clean such surfaces after service.

Cleanliness also extends to your personal hygiene. Make sure your hair is tied and that you're wearing hair nets when serving food. Have your employees wear gloves when serving food. If wearing gloves is impractical, they need to have clean nails, and they need to wash their hands regularly. Do not allow sick employees into your kitchen since they'll end up infecting everyone. The food industry is particularly bad with this but, thankfully, this attitude is changing.

Don't show up to work if you're sick as well. You might lose income during the days you're sick but it's better to rest and return healthy rather than push yourself and churn out substandard food. Your customers will notice the difference in taste and you could also end up infecting them with whatever you're carrying.

Hazardous Food Processes

Meat, poultry, and seafood are potentially hazardous foods and inspectors will make sure they're being handled properly. It isn't just handling, they need to be stored and cooked at the right temperatures as well to avoid food poisoning. As long as you've educated yourself and your employees about proper food handling procedures and are practicing them, you won't have any issues with this.

Make sure these foods are stored properly as described previously. Temperature and labeling are crucial and inspectors will check these in detail.

Knowledge

An area that most food truck operators fall short is food safety knowledge. While operators themselves might know all the regulations, they fail to ensure their employees know them as well. Inspectors will quiz you and your staff about them during inspections so you need to make sure they're educated in all aspects of it.

Inspectors will ask your staff about cooking and storage methods. Expect them to also ask you about the temperature measurement tools and their calibration. Here are some of the other aspects of food preparation your employees will be asked about:

- Procedures that limit bare-hand contact with cooked food
- How often employees use gloves and wash their hands
- Documentation with regards to reporting illnesses and injuries. Drafting a policy beforehand and prominently displaying it is a good practice to follow.
- Pest control measures
- Training procedures for new employees and training managers' certifications. Only someone who's qualified in food safety knowledge should train new employees.
- Hazardous food handling procedures
- Food labeling and review procedures

- Salad ingredients preparation. Where produce is washed and the cleanliness of that area will be inspected. They'll also check whether produce is being mixed with raw food.

Preparing for an Inspection

The mere mention of a health inspection is enough to send restaurant and food truck owners into a tizzy. It can be stressful, so it's best to be prepared beforehand and to make food safety an ingrained process in your business. It's a good idea to run inspection drills by yourself so that your employees are used to maintaining high standards at the workplace. If you're serious about food safety, your employees will follow suit.

Here are the areas you need to focus on.

Food Prep and Storage

Check to see if all food on the truck is safe for consumption. Raw meat and cooked food should not be in contact with one another. All containers should be labeled properly with dates on them. It's also a good idea to include the expiry date on the container so that you won't have to open it to know what's inside. Food should not be left exposed for lengthy amounts of time in the prep area.

All food should be stored at proper temperatures. This is especially the case with meat and dairy products, whether raw or cooked. Food that is cooked hot should not be refrigerated immediately. Let it cool down and store it safely. Products that customers use must be sanitized and must be stored properly, away from raw food and food undergoing preparation.

Employee Behavior

Everyone who cooks food must use meat thermometers to make sure it's well cooked. Every employee must also wash their hands regularly and properly. Make sure you demonstrate proper handwashing techniques to employees. Have new employees go through a rigorous training process so that they learn proper procedures. Ask them about food safety practices regularly and test them.

They need to be wearing appropriate clothing that protects them and shields food from them. Hair must be tied and employees must follow proper hygiene. Their personal items should be securely stored and should not be present in food preparation areas.

Equipment Health

You'll be using a lot of equipment such as fridges, freezers and thermometers. Make sure you monitor their temperatures and conditions regularly. Carry out preemptive maintenance regularly so that you don't risk a breakdown or disruption of service. All cleaning chemicals should be kept well away from food preparation areas and stored separately. Once they're used you and your employees must sanitize yourselves thoroughly.

There must be at least one designated sink for handwashing purposes only. The truck's ventilation systems must work well and all fire management systems must be in working order. Some jurisdictions limit the number of activities that can be performed in a truck, so make sure you're using a commercial kitchen for performing these.

Cleanliness

Make sure everything is spotless and that your truck is in good condition. Dirty dishes should be stored and washed as required and there shouldn't be any sign of pests. You need to have proper garbage and waste disposal systems installed. The truck's exterior also needs to be cleaned thoroughly.

Papers

Make sure all of your permits and paperwork is in order and that you have your records in order. You should be able to pull maintenance and cleanliness records easily on demand.

When the time comes to run your inspection make sure you run it randomly and conduct it as a rigorous formal process. This further drills the message into your employees that you're extremely serious about food safety and that you won't accept shortcuts. Visit your local government office to learn more about how the inspectors will carry out their inspections.

If you want to, you can even have a friend come by and perform a "surprise" check on your truck so that your employees are kept on their toes. Make sure everything is examined and has high standards. Ensuring food safety is a matter of culture. You cannot prepare for it over the course of a day or two days. Good practices result from consistency and proper training. Invest in these resources constantly.

Make it a point to review the results of your inspection with your employees. Highlight what needs to be improved and what your team is doing well. Remember that the objective of this exercise is to educate your employees, not intimidate them. They need to understand that food safety is a critical issue, and that it needs to become second nature for your business. If someone isn't performing a task in the right manner, explain what needs to be corrected. Provide positive encouragement and your team will respond appropriately.

You need to let your staff know the consequences of failing a health inspection. You don't want them to think that some of their missteps were small and that they aren't a big deal. This is the wrong attitude to have and will torpedo your business. Reward them when they rectify previously incorrect processes. It's a good idea to get them thinking in terms of team work. If any member performs poorly, the entire team has to be held accountable (including yourself.) If every task is performed well, reward the whole team with a night off or schedule some fun event everyone can take part in.

The frequency of your self-inspection is up to you but it's good to run it every other week. Your employees will grumble but don't let this stop you. It's your business and the better prepared you are the more successful you'll be. You'll avoid serious violations that will put everyone at risk.

Be prepared and you'll have nothing to worry about

Chapter 10:

How to Grow, Expand, and Ensure

a Bright Future

At first, your food truck is going to be staffed primarily by your friends and family. You might have a cousin help you with the grill, and one of your friends might man the commercial kitchen to make sure everything runs smoothly there. For long-term success, you need to move away from the DIY approach and hire employees. It's more difficult to enforce stringent standards on your friends and family since you know them personally.

You'll find it hard to separate personal-time and business-time and this will strain your relationships if it goes on for long. This is why you need to hire employees as quickly as possible. Of course, you need to make sure that you can afford to hire them. The good news is that the average food truck operation doesn't need many employees.

The size of your truck determines how many on-site employees you will need. Most trucks require two to three people to operate smoothly. One of these people will be you so that leaves you with two employees. One employee helps you in the kitchen and another can be the quasi front-of-the-house staff. This person can manage lines and keep customers happy. They can help collect payment when lines get long and can also engage with customers to make sure your marketing efforts are striking the right chord with them.

Given the marketing focused role to the front-end person, you can have your social media manager man this role. However, if your ordering window is well organized you won't necessarily need a staff member out in front. Evaluate which method provides your customers with the best experience and stick with that. You'll be working out of a commercial kitchen as well, and local laws will dictate which cooking processes get executed in it.

You might have to hire a person to handle that kitchen in between service times to make sure food is ready to go once you arrive. This is especially the case if you're working two spots during the day. This employee can arrive in the afternoon (during your first shift), prep the food in the kitchen and help you serve it in the evening. That way, the employee who helped you in the truck during the first service gets a break. You don't get one but then again, you're the owner!

As your business matures, there are a few roles you might want to consider hiring employees for. These are:

- Order takers/ Service window attendants
- Cooks
- Driver
- Kitchen workers
- Business manager

A business manager will come in handy when you're looking to expand your operation. I'll deal with the specifics of this later in this chapter.

Hiring Staff

You want to hire good people who will be assets to your business. The key to attracting great employees is to be a great employer. Before you think of hiring people, sit down and think about what you have to offer. Put yourself in the shoes of someone who's looking to work and ask yourself what this person would gain working for you. Almost everyone needs a steady stream of encouragement and guidance. They also want to work reasonable hours and receive above-average pay.

Take some time to think about the requirements of the job you're advertising for. Some jobs will have physical requirements. If you're hiring a cook or a chef, you want someone who has experience with your cuisine. If you think you can train someone then this is up to you as well. Keep in mind that it'll take a trainee chef a while to rise to a position where they can run the kitchen themselves. If your objective is to take a step back, this isn't going to happen soon with this sort of a hire.

Whichever role you're hiring for, you'll want your employees to be respectful and courteous. I'm not talking about just towards the customer but also towards you and the other members of your team. Team is the keyword here. You don't want employees who cannot function as a part of one unit. Everyone needs to lean on and count on one another, that's the only way your business is going to succeed.

There are different ways of evaluating an employee and this depends on the role they'll play. An interview is the standard but, unfortunately, it tells you next to nothing about them. Some people don't interview well, while others know how to appear "correct" during interviews only to drop the facade once hired. Try to get as many real world examples from them as possible, and don't let your emotions sway you too much. Conduct background checks on them and check with their references. If you're hiring a chef, it's common to put them through a cooking test.

The best way to evaluate them is to give them cheap ingredients and ask them to come up with something that can be turned into a profit.

The best chefs have a knack of selecting cheap ingredients and turning them into multiple dishes so your profit margins increase. They should also understand the ethos behind your menu and should suggest improvement and possible changes to it. You want someone who is ambitious and is looking to make a mark. A chef of a successful food truck business gains a lot of coverage, so make sure you're looking at someone who's in it for the food, not just the fame.

Training

Good employees cannot help you unless they're well-trained. Many food truck owners neglect to train their employees and this is unfortunate. Hiring an employee and leaving them to themselves will lead to feelings of resentment. Show them how to do their job well and make sure they're well-trained with regards to food handling procedures. Even non-food handling employees must be aware of proper procedures. After all, food is the beating heart of the business and everyone must be aware of what's necessary.

You must also educate them on the culture of your business. Your employees, all of them, need to know what goes into each and every dish on the menu, and they need to have tasted it. Customers will ask them what an item tastes like, and they need to be able to convey this information well. Let them know of which items they need to push and how they need to structure orders during rush time.

Every menu should have one or two items that are delicious and that can be prepared well in advance without compromising their taste. When lines start to get longer, selling these items reduces pressure on the kitchen and makes service more manageable. Your employees need to be aware of when they need to start pushing these items and work as partners with the kitchen.

Health codes and storage requirements are essential training elements. Cleaning and after service tasks should also be detailed. This is where you get to enforce standards and you can set an example. Show your employees how work needs to be carried out, and they'll do it. Show them tardiness and other poor habits and that's what they'll follow. Lead by example, not with words.

Create a Manual

It's tedious work, but make sure you create an operations and training manual. Write out all of your processes in detail and make sure every employee follows them appropriately. The best part about a manual is that it creates consistency in your business and provides everyone with a handy reference in case of disputes. It's easier to enforce standards once something is written down. Once your business grows, having a manual makes it easy for you to expand to other locations and franchisees.

At the very least, your manual needs to outline:

- Code of conduct and expected standards of behavior
- Kitchen processes
- Purchasing and inventory control processes
- Training methods
- Commercial kitchen processes
- Food safety practices
    - Storage
    - Instruments
    - Labeling
    - Monitoring
    - Day to day tasks
- Equipment maintenance
- Vehicle maintenance tasks
- Parking and cleaning tasks
- Vehicle breakdown processes

We've been looking at the food side of the business throughout the book but remember that you're also operating a vehicle. This is a commercial vehicle and it needs regular maintenance. You'll need to regularly check its air filter and also check whether it needs an oil change. Perform maintenance on it regularly, and make sure everything is in working order.

As the biggest asset your business has, you also need to make sure it's cleaned regularly and that all of your employees know what to do in case the truck breaks down. Have a list of emergency contacts on hand and distribute this list to all of your employees so that the right people can be contacted immediately. Finding a good mechanic is crucial. Check with other food truck owners about this. If you bought the vehicle from a dealer, they'll know who the good mechanics are. Food truck associations also maintain lists of such tradespeople.

Ensuring Long-Term Success

The food truck business is a tough one but it's fully possible for you to be successful. Success is a collection of habits, instead of a result. Many food truck owners hope and wish for it but never take the time to sit down and develop processes that will ensure they're successful. Here are a few tips that will help you along the road to success.

Adapt

Your business and marketing plan aren't set in stone. Conditions change and your business needs to adapt with them. People's taste in food will change so you need to always ensure your menu remains fresh and that you're providing your customers with the highest value. When it comes to marketing, the demographics of your ideal customer will change. Your customer base 10 years from now will not be the same as it is today.

They'll use different technology, and they'll expect different levels of service. Adapting is the key to long-term success.

Have Capital Reserves

Here's a piece of advice that some people won't like and will ignore. The ones who follow it will obtain success. Have a year's worth of capital in the bank when starting out. You're not going to be an overnight success so having this excess cash parked in the bank will help you build consistency and won't leave you starving during lean months. You never know when unexpected events might occur so always prepare for them.

Have cash reserves equal to six months expenses in the bank at all times. This will help you deal with unexpected events quickly and you won't have to let go of your employees.

Have a Grand Opening

Drum up as much enthusiasm as possible for your opening. Let everyone know when you're going to begin and coordinate all of your marketing to this event. Making yourself a big deal is important because that's how your customers will treat you.

Lead by Example

As I mentioned earlier, your employees won't follow your words, but they'll follow your example. You cannot expect to behave discourteously and magically expect your employees to behave well.

Go Local and Provide Great Service

The secret of your success is to focus your marketing and service efforts locally. National coverage won't matter because people in far-flung places cannot order food from you. Instill and promote local pride through everything you do and people will flock to you.

Keep Your Employees Happy and Build Trust

The key to a successful business is happy employees. This doesn't mean you give into their every whim. Employees are happiest when their positions are secure and when you can assure them that their salaries will always be paid on time. Security is extremely important to them. Trust them to execute their jobs once you've given them the right training. Provide support but allow them the flexibility to own the processes they're responsible for.

Be Consistent

Consistency in service, processes, and professionalism is the key to success. Your customers will come to expect a certain level of service with your business. Provide them with terrible service and this is what they'll expect. You'll also attract the kind of customer that doesn't care about service and you'll find your business suffers as a result. Practice consistency in everything and you'll build a true asset.

Communicate

Your employees and customers aren't mind readers. You need to communicate properly to them. Make your instructions explicit and don't leave anything up in the air. Some owners communicate by suggestion and this is an especially ineffective way to communicate. Be explicit with your communication.

When it comes to customers, maintain your tone throughout your marketing channels. Seek feedback from them and engage with them online. The more human you are, the more they'll flock to you.

Monitor Costs

It's important to make money, but before that, you need to monitor costs. You don't want to cut them down to the bone and sacrifice quality. However, you need to keep them at realistic levels.

Growing Your Business

Establishing one successful food truck is great but it's possible for you to expand this single truck to a successful franchise. There are different ways you can expand your business. The first is to consider opening another truck and franchising your business. Make sure your franchising agreements are air-tight. You don't want to lose control of your business. Franchising is a great way to create passive income streams and let someone else do the work while you earn royalties on your asset.

Another expansion option is to start a brick and mortar restaurant. You can use the goodwill you generated from your truck to drive customers to a fixed location. Running a restaurant is a tough business so make sure you understand all the consequences of getting into it.

Whichever option you choose, make sure you create a solid business plan that follows the principles outlined earlier in this book. Follow the same steps and you'll have a successful business expansion. Don't expand too fast and borrow too much money to fund expansion. Many businesses fail due to expanding too quickly. Take it slowly and move at a pace that is comfortable for you.

Conclusion

Do you still want to start a food truck? It's true that they offer a lower cost entry option into the food service business than a full-blown restaurant. However, lower costs don't mean lower levels of difficulty. You'll face a lot of the same challenges that restaurant owners face and you'll need every ounce of strength you have to make sure your business is successful. Put in the effort and you'll realize the rewards.

What are the rewards on offer? For starters, a successful business that can secure you and your family's financial future. A great food truck business is an asset that you can turn into bigger and better cash flows for yourself. You can even start secondary lines of business while your truck is running. For example, you can launch a line on your own sauces and condiments.

You could start a catering business for large events as well. The possibilities are endless. Many food truck owners sell merchandise and partner with local businesses to create special products that customers love. There are many locations that a food truck business works in, and as you become more experienced, you'll be able to identify which ones work and which ones don't.

The first month or two will be rocky because there's a lot for you to learn. However, once you master those initial hurdles, you'll find that the business is extremely rewarding and is a great long-term option for you. Install right processes and expectations and you'll earn all your rewards.

I'm positive you now have a clear roadmap to starting your own food truck journey. I wish you all the luck in the world with your business. Do let me know what you think of this book by leaving me a review on Amazon!

References

25 Powerful Food Truck Industry Statistics in 2020. (2020, January 30). 2ndKitchen. https://2ndkitchen.com/restaurants/food-truck-statistics/

Buy the Insurance You Need for Your Food Truck Business. (2020, September 30). Dummies. https://www.dummies.com/business/start-a-business/buy-the-insurance-you-need-for-your-food-truck-business/

Crook, I. (2019, June 6). *Food Truck Marketing Plan: Strategies to Supercharge Your Business.* AppInstitute. https://appinstitute.com/food-truck-marketing-plan/.

Here Are Need-To-Know Food Truck Costs (and How to Save Money). (2020, September 30). Square. https://squareup.com/us/en/townsquare/food-truck-cost?country_redirection=true

Hints for Building Your Food Truck Menu. (2020, September 30). Dummies. https://www.dummies.com/business/start-a-business/hints-for-building-your-food-truck-menu/

How to Start a Food Truck 19: Organize Your Licenses and Permits. (2020, May 28). FoodTruckr | How to Start and Run a Successful Food Truck Business. https://foodtruckr.com/2020/05/start-food-truck-19-organize-licenses-permits

How To Start A Food Truck Business: A Cost Breakdown - Innovative ideas & solutions. (2018, May 11). Innovative Ideas & Solutions. https://posbistro.com/blog/how-to-start-food-truck-cost-breakdown/

Restaurant Profitability and Failure Rates: What You Need to Know | FSR magazine. (2019). FSR Magazine.

https://www.fsrmagazine.com/expert-takes/restaurant-profitability-and-failure-rates-what-you-need-know

Image References

battery. (2020). In *pixabay*.

burger-van. (2020). In *pixabay*.

city-busan-busa. (2020). In *pixabay*.

disneyland. (2020). In *pixabay*.

e-military-coffee. (2020). In *pixabay*.

fall-season. (2020). In *pixabay*.

food-festival. (2020). In *pixabay*.

hamburger. (2020). In *pixabay*.

ice-cream-dessert-van-. (2020). In *pixabay*.

ice-cream-truck. (2020). In *pixabay*.

intage-citroën. (2020). In *pixabay*.

new-york-humor. (2020). In *pixabay*.

oldtimer. (2020). In *pixabay*.

power-supply-car-purple. (2020). In *pixabay*.

roadsign. (2020). In *pixabay*.

skyscraper. (2020). In *pixabay*.

taco-food-truck. (2020). In *pixabay*.

verkoopwagen. (2020). In *pixabay*.

vintage-food. (2020). In *pixabay*.

CPSIA information can be obtained
at www.ICGtesting.com
Printed in the USA
BVHW091409210422
634952BV00005B/167